THE SECOND WORLD WAR

1945

JOHN CHRISTOPHER & CAMPBELL McCUTCHEON

AMBERLEY

First published 2015

Amberley Publishing
The Hill, Stroud
Gloucestershire, GL5 4EP

www.amberley-books.com

British Library Cataloguing in Publication Data.
A catalogue record for this book is available from the British Library.

ISBN 978 1 4456 2215 6 (print)
ISBN 978 1 4456 2231 6 (ebook)

Typeset in 11pt on 15pt Sabon.
Typesetting and Origination by Amberley Publishing.
Printed in the UK.

Contents

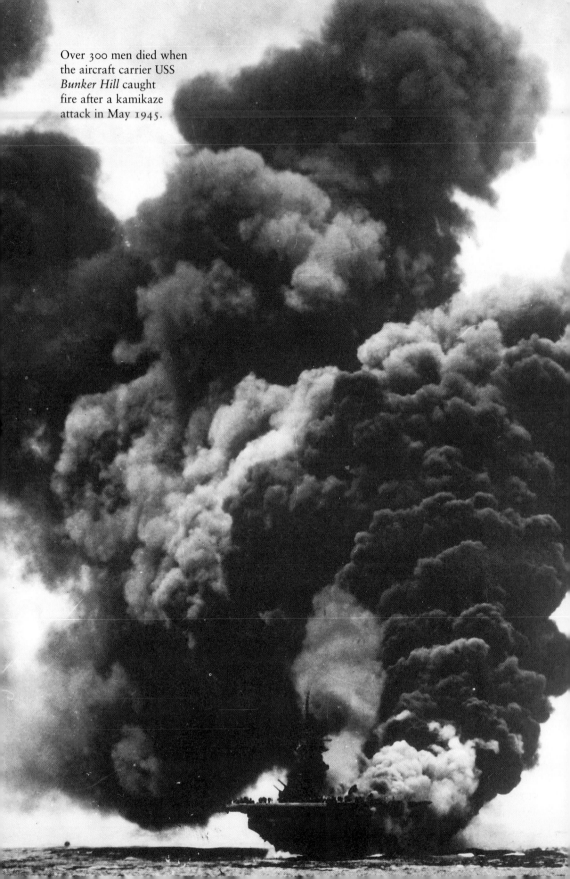

Over 300 men died when the aircraft carrier USS *Bunker Hill* caught fire after a kamikaze attack in May 1945.

A Brave New World

The economic might of the United States and the numerical superiority of the Soviet Union provided a relentless tide of tanks, ships, aircraft, munitions and men and it was these that would end the war in favour of the Allies. Japan had known in 1941 that she would have to knock out the American fighting capability quickly so that peace could be sued for on Japanese terms. They failed at the first hurdle, and for them the war was one of decline and disaster from 1942 onwards. The German invasion of Russia, Operation Barbarossa, was the beginning of the end of the Axis forces in Europe. The awakening of the Russian 'Bear' saw millions of Germans and their allies die on the Steppes of Russia as they were eventually forced back to the Fatherland itself. Despite the Ardennes offensive, and its slim victories, Germany was all but finished, its reserves used up and on the defensive on all fronts. Japanese forces were being forced back to the mainland of Japan itself. The war would end soon, but the public did not know just how dramatic the final end would be.

On 1 January 1945, the Russians are in Czechoslovakia. The German Army Group Centre, holding the last foreign-based economic and industrial centre in German control, is under attack by 850,000 Soviet soldiers, with around 10,000 artillery pieces, nearly 600 tanks and 1,400 aircraft. The Germans can muster 550,000 men, 5,000 artillery pieces and 700 aircraft. With a numerical superiority of some two to one, the Russians push through the German troops slowly but steadily. Despite early successes in the Ardennes, the Germans have overstretched themselves. They attack the US Seventh Army in Alsace Lorraine, at the Colmar Pocket. The Americans retreat but hold Strasbourg. The Americans lose 15,600 soldiers, with German losses totaling 25,000. In Burma, Chinese units link up but the meet major resistance from the Japanese 56th Division. The war has seen many technological advances and, on 2 January, the Americans use a Sikorsky helicopter on convoy duties for the very first time. On the night of 3/4 January, the American 3rd Fleet attacks Formosa, with 100 Japanese aircraft destroyed. A final attack on Bastogne is made by the Germans on 3 January. The Allies have had time to prepare and now counterattack. The US First attacks the north of the bulge and the US Third attacks the bottom. The Germans begin to withdraw to Houffalize on 8 January but they are forced further east under the American onslaught. The US Third and First meet at Houffalize on 16 January.

In Burma, General William Slim's forces land unopposed on Akyab on 4 January, capturing the airfield, as well as the port. In a desperate effort to stop landings at Luzon, Philippines, the Japanese launch suicide attacks on the US 7th Fleet. Around 1,000 Americans and Australians are killed, a minesweeper is sunk and around thirty other vessels are damaged between 4–6 January. In an effort to stop the American onslaught in the Ardennes, the Luftwaffe launch Operation Bodenplatte, using 1,035 aircraft to attack Allied airfields in Belgium and Holland. Despite destroying 156 aircraft, the Germans lose 277. It is a last-ditch effort and many of the German reserves are thrown at the Allies. They make no further major offensive raids in the war. The Germans attack in Hungary, capturing Esztergom on 7 January. After a heavy bombardment, Luzon is invaded unopposed on 9 January. Knowing that their country will soon be taken by the Soviets, Czech partisans rise up on 10 January, harassing the Germans and attacking supply lines. Poland sees the start of the Vistula-Oder offensive too, with the Russians sending 2 million men into action. East Prussia is attacked on 13 January and tanks have reached Sochaczew on 17 January. In Burma, the Irrawaddy is crossed by the 19th Division on 14 January. They meet stiff resistance but hold their bridgehead.

The Allies counterattack after the Battle of the Bulge, with forays into the Roermond area and up the Roer river valley from 15 to 26 January. The Chinese secure the Burma Road on 16 January, having occupied Namhkan. Between 18 and 27 January, the Germans attack towards Budapest but fail to get closer than 15 miles from the city on 22 January. The Soviets counterattack on the 27th and attempts to reach Budapest have failed. The Japanese are in retreat in Burma, but this does not stop an all-out battle at Namhpakka between 18 January and 3 February. Krakow is liberated on 19 January by the Soviet 1st Ukrainian Front. They have surrounded the German Third and Fourth Panzer Armies, which are now isolated in East Prussia.

The island of Ramree sees the British 71st Brigade land unopposed on 21 January. However, as the British troops head inland, they meet stiffer and stiffer resistance and it takes until mid-February to clear the island, giving the Allies a perfect base for more long-range attacks on Rangoon. On the Vistula river, the Germans are trapped the east bank on 23 January, having had all of the road and rail bridges cut across the river. Brombarg, an important part of the Poznan defensive line, is captured on the same day. The true horror of Nazism is brought home on 27 January when Auschwitz-Birkenau is liberated. The camp has been abandoned since 18 January, with only a few hundred of the weakest captives left after the SS evacuates 20,000 and marches them towards the west. The Burma Road reopens on the same day and it is possible to supply China again. After 100,000 casualties on the German side, and 82,400 American and British casualties, the Battle of the Bulge is finally over, with a massive German defeat. They have also lost around 1,000 aircraft and 800 tanks. While the Allies have lost similar numbers of equipment, theirs can easily be replaced in a month or so. The knocking out of so many weapons

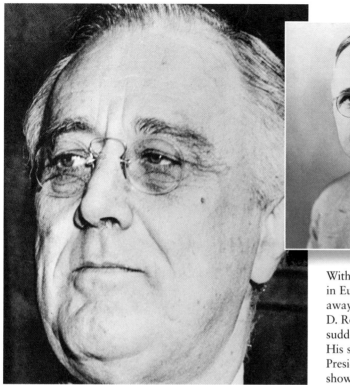

With an end to the conflict in Europe only months away, US President Franklin D. Roosevelt, *left*, died suddenly on 12 April 1945. His successor was the Vice President, Harry S. Truman, shown above.

and the trained men that operated them is fatal to the Germans. Between 28 January and 1 February, the Americans attack near St Vith, advancing through the German defences, despite opposition. On 29 January, another unopposed landing is made near Bataan, Philippines. On the next day, the Soviets make bridgeheads across the Oder river, having advanced over 350 miles, liberating Poland and much of Czechoslovakia, and are now some 100 miles from Berlin. Over that 355 miles lie 500,000 dead, wounded or captured Germans, along with 1,300 aircraft, 1,400 tanks and around 14,000 artillery weapons. In the Philippines, the Americans land at Nasugbu Bay, around 50 miles from Manila.

February begins with a breakout by the German Fourth Army, which is trapped in East Prussia. Their attack towards Elbing fails and they succumb to the Russians. Around 17,000 Japanese troops defend Manila, and the Philippines capital is attacked by the Americans on 3 March. It takes a month to capture the city, and the Japanese garrison is wiped out but not before the city is destroyed. Only 1,000 Americans are killed, with 5,500 wounded, but most of the 17,000 Japanese troops are killed along with 100,000 civilians. Roosevelt, Stalin and Churchill meet at Yalta between 4–11 February. It is here that the real planning for the end of the war begins, with agreement made that Germany is to be split into four zones, and Austria will be too. It is agreed that Soviet Russia will declare war on Japan two months after the end of the war in

Above: 'And now the chatter-bug.' With an end to the war so close, it was important to maintain the will to get the job done. This British newspaper cartoon by Illingworth presents a German 'gremlin' in the form of a chatter-bug undermining effort on the Home Front.

Europe. The Soviets also plan to annex parts of Poland into Russian territory. The Colmar Pocket is split on 5 February. Elimination of the German forces here will make the crossing of the Rhine possible. Lower Silesia is captured between 8 and 24 February, and 115,000 Russians and other foreign nationals are freed. On 9 February, von Rundstedt finally convinces Hitler to evacuate the German troops in the Colmar Pocket, leaving no Germans on the western banks of the Rhine south of Strasbourg. An attack by the Russians against the German Second Army near Sepolno, Poland, is thwarted and Russian progress is interminably slow. 30,000 Axis troops are surrounded in Budapest and on 11 February they attempt to break out. Barely 700 Hungarian and German troops manage to escape. Dresden is bombed on the evening of 13/14 February, with 805 bombers jettisoning their loads of bombs on the city, creating a huge firestorm, which kills 50,000 inhabitants. Dresden has no strategic value and is bombed only as part of Bomber Command's plan to bring fear into the civilian population and end the war early. The USAAF attacks on the morning of 14 February, adding to the death and destruction. The displacement of Germans in East Prussia reaches 1.2 million, who have fled west. Some have gone by land, others by sea, although British and Russian forces have killed many thousands in the sinking of ships on the dangerous route to northern Germany.

In the Philippines, the Japanese are being cleared from manila Bay. Between 16 and 28 February, Bataan falls, as does Corregidor. At Corregidor, the Japanese fight to the death. The bombardment of Iwo Jima begins on 16 February, with the objective ultimately the capture of the island. It is three hours' flying time from Tokyo on mainland Japan. There are 21,000 Japanese on Iwo Jima and, while initial landings on 17 February are lightly contested, the defenders soon bring down a hail of shells on the American invaders. Despite this, the Americans land 30,000 troops on Iwo Jima at the end of day one. General Slim's troops began their break out from the Irrawaddy on 21 February and head for Mandalay. In the north of the country, the Japanese are on the retreat near Myitson, after a three-day battle in the area. The Roer river in Germany is crossed on 23 February and Allied troops head for the Rhine. With the Canadians attacking Goch on 21 February, German reserves are committed in the north and there are none left for this southern attack and by nightfall, 28 divisions have crossed the Roer. The south of Iwo Jima is taken on 23 February, with the iconic view of the American flag-raising being photographed then. The battle for the north of the island rages! Syria declares war on Germany on 26 February, with Saudi Arabia following on 28 February. The Americans cross the Rhine and head into Germany proper, while in Palawan, the Americans capture the island on 28 February.

An offensive begins on 1 March as the 1st Belorussian Front attacks the German Third Panzer Army. The 203,000 Germans have 700 tanks and 2,500 artillery pieces. The attack is a prelude to the push on Berlin and is intended to give the Russians some protection on their flank. With a blizzard blowing, Patton's Third Army attacks across the Kyll river in France on 3 March on its

Above: The Allies' strategic bombing campaign had reduced the streets of many German towns and cities to featureless canyons of rubble. This is Nuremberg, with the twin-spired Lorenz Church in the distance. *(US DoD)*

While conventional bombing had left much of Europe in ruins, the dawn of nuclear warfare raised the stakes to an unimaginable level. The dropping of Atomic bombs on the cities of Hiroshima and Nagasaki, shown left, might have brought the war against Japan to an early close, but the post-war stand-off between West and East saw the world on the brink of destruction through Mutually Assured Destruction, otherwise known as MAD.

way to the Rhine. In the east, the German Fourth Panzer Army attacks across the Oder but the Russians stop them with superior firepower. The first B-29s land on Iwo Jima, after the airfield was prepared for them. Tokyo is but a few hours away now. The Germans attack in Hungary on 6 March, trying to recapture the oilfields at Nagykanizsa and Budapest. In Yugoslavia, Marshall Tito forms a provisional government on 7 March.

The Ludendorff Bridge at Remagen is captured intact on 7 March. Despite attack from the air and shelling, as well as attempts to demolish the bridge, it manages to stay up for a further ten days before collapsing into the Rhine. The west bank of the Rhine has been cleared of Germans by 10 March, with the loss of 112,000 soldiers, 90,000 of those on the German side. 100,000 die in Tokyo on 10 March as the Americans unleash a firestorm on the Japanese capital. It is the first raid from Iwo Jima and it destroys 16 square miles of Tokyo. The Siegfried Line is circumvented when Patton's Third Army crosses the Moselle on 14 March. In Hungary, on 16 March, the Hungarian Third Army is routed as the Russians attack between Lake Velencei and Bicske. Iwo Jima is finally declared free of Japanese after twenty-six days of fighting that see only 1,083 Japanese survive out of 21,000 defenders. The Americans lose 6,821 dead. The road to Mandalay is clear and the Allies begin the battle for the Burmese city on 17 March. The main Japanese garrison is at Fort Dufferin and this is pounded from the air and by British artillery for two days, causing the Japanese to evacuate on 19 March. The Americans continue their island hopping campaign and take Panay, in the Philippines, on 19 March, with Guimaras Island following straight after. By 20 March, no German fighting forces remain on the east bank of the Oder river and Altdamm is captured.

The Rhine is finally crossed in Germany on 22 March. Bridgeheads are made at Nierstein and Oppenheim, with a whole division across the river by the next day. Montgomery crosses on the 23rd with the 21st Army group. There are 1.25 million men in this army and they cross in numerous places. German resistance is low as the German soldiers are utterly exhausted after the battles on the west bank of the Rhine. Chinese troops on two fronts meet in northern Burma, bringing to an end the campaign there on 24 March. In Hungary, the war is also coming to a close as Hungarian troops begin to desert in droves. By 28 March, the Russians are on the Austrian border. Danzig falls to the Red Army on 30 March. 10,000 troops, sailors and 45 submarines are captured.

April Fool's Day sees the invasion of Okinawa. Around 183,000 American troops begin to land, unopposed, as the Japanese have withdrawn to a defensive line behind Shuri. The 80,000 Japanese are dug in and prepared. Okinawa is 325 miles from Japan, has two airfields and two bays suitable for the amassing of the hundreds of ships needed to make the final assault on the Japanese mainland. The Ruhr is encircled between 2 and 3 April when Allied forces meet at Lippstadt. Holland has been largely bypassed and the Allies begin the operation to clear the country of Nazis on 4 April. The Dutch are running out of food and it is important that this is done quickly, leaving the way open to attack northern Germany. On 5 April, the Czechs announce the Czech Republic at Kosice, calling on all Czechs and Slovaks to rise up against the Germans. The world's largest battleship, the *Yamamoto*, is sunk by US warplanes on 7 April while on the way to Okinawa to attack the US invasion forces. *Yamamoto* has just enough fuel to reach the island and is on a suicide mission. Another American success that day is when the USAAF sends P-51 fighters to escort the B-29s all the way to Japan. American forces come up against the Japanese defenders on the Shuri Line on 9 April, and meet stiff resistance. In northern Italy, the final push in the north is underway on the night of 9 April. The US Fifth and British Eighth Armies attack on the Po river at the Argenta Gap. Aerial bombardments and five artillery barrages soften the German defenders and by the morning of 10 April, the Allies are crossing the Senino river in three places.

10 April sees the British Fourteenth Army head for Rangoon before the monsoons start in mid-May and before the Japanese can construct an effective defensive line in front of the Burmese capital. Magdeburg is taken without a fight on 11 April as the German army in the west begins to collapse. President Roosevelt dies on 12 April of a cerebral haemorrhage. Harry S. Truman takes over as president. Vienna is liberated on 13 April. Dwight D. Eisenhower informs the Allies that the capture of Berlin takes second place to the capture of Norway and Denmark, and the securing of the southern flanks of the Allied advance. In Italy, an offensive begins by the US Fifth Army on 14 April. An attack is made between Montese and Vergato.

On 16 April, the final push by the Soviets towards Berlin begins. In three parts, the Soviet plan is to attack over the Oder and Neisse rivers, splitting and isolating the many German units before Berlin, capturing the city and then heading for the Elbe river. There are 2.5 million Russian and Polish soldiers facing the million Germans, who are made up of regular soldiers, home guard and police detachments. The Germans are outnumbered in equipment too. Facing their 1,500 tanks are 6,250. Their 3,300 aircraft are outnumbered by 7,500 Russian fighters and bombers and their 10,400 artillery pieces are outnumbered by 41,600 Russian weapons. A push is also being made in the Argenta Gap on the same day and the British Eighth Army makes it over the Fossa Marina canal, and have breached the German lines. The Argenta Gap is open!

In the Philippines, on 17 April, the American X Corps has landed on Mindanao as part of their policy of picking each island off one by one. On 18 April, the last shots are fired in the Ruhr and upwards of 370,000 prisoners are captured by the Allies. In the Netherlands, the Germans have been surrounded in the west of the country. Split from the rest of the Axis forces, they will soon be without food and ammunition. After five days of hard fighting, Nuremburg falls to the US Third Army on 20 April. The noose is tightening and the Russian 1st Belorussian Front has knocked out most of the German opposition on the Oder and is heading for Berlin. The Russians want to encircle German troops south-east of Berlin so they cannot escape to the city and bolster its defences. This action also helps prevent units escaping from Berlin. Those still in the city are effectively trapped by 24 April. Hitler has decided to remain in the city to organise its defence, rather than escape to his redoubt in the Wolf's Lair.

The Argenta Gap is open and the Germans are in full retreat, abandoning much of their heavy equipment, while being harried by the British and South African troops chasing them. On 23 April, the last German resistance in the Harz Mountains surrenders, while Hamburg has been reached by the British Second Army. Berlin is totally encircled by 25 April and heavy air raids and artillery bombardment pummel the city on 26 April. Attacks on the city begin later in the day. Attacks are made from all parts of the city. The suburbs are soon conquered. The assault on the Reichstag begins on 28 April. Holland effectively surrenders on 28 April too. The civilian population are starving and the German Reichskommissar agrees to let the Allies supply food and coal to the Dutch in exchange for the Allies not pushing further east. It is the end of fighting in the country. In Italy the Germans are in a full scale rout and Mussolini is captured, along with his wife, while trying to escape to Austria as the puppet state collapses in the north. He and his wife are shot and their bodies strung up in the Piazzale Loretto, Milan. Hitler, now effectively trapped in the Führer Bunker, orders the arrest of Himmler, who has tried to negotiate with the Allies. Hermann Goering has already been replaced by Ritter von Greim, who has been ordered to escape from Berlin to arrest Himmler. Hitler, now effectively going mad, marries his long time mistress, Eva Braun, on 29 April. Admiral Karl Doenitz is nominated as his successor.

German forces in Italy effectively surrender on 2 May. The agreement to make a ceasefire is made on 29 April after much discussion between the SS commander in Italy and the head of the OSS in Switzerland. This saves much of Italy's industry from destruction under Hitler's scorched earth policy. The German forces in Frankfurt-an-der-Oder try to break out to make for Berlin but are utterly destroyed. 60,000 soldiers are killed and 120,000 taken into captivity by the Soviets. In Holland, the RAF drops food to civilians in efforts to prevent starvation. Using Lancaster bombers, they drop containers of food and heating equipment. Hitler and Eva Braun commit suicide on 30 April. Adolf Hitler shoots himself, while Braun takes poison. Their bodies are cremated by the SS but theories about his death persist to this day.

With the death of their leader, the Germans in Berlin try to negotiate a surrender but the Soviets demand unconditional surrender. The fighting continues. In Burma, the Gurkhas land by air at Elephant Point, close to Rangoon. They soon capture the area, opening the way for amphibious landings up the Rangoon river. In the rush to control parts of Germany, the British reach Wismar, preventing the Russians entering Schleswig-Holstein. After a three-day battle, the Reichstag falls on 2 May. 2,500 of the defenders have been killed, with many of the remaining 2,500 injured. The Russians place their flag on top of the government building. The city surrenders. Russian casualties in the fight for Berlin are 300,000, with 2,000 tanks lost. Around one million Germans have been killed or captured. In Burma, Allied victories see the Indian 20th Division capture Prome, preventing Japanese retreat from the Arakan. On 3 May, Rangoon is captured, almost without a shot being fired. The city, however, has suffered from the intensive bombing in the preceding months. All of north-western Germany is in Allied control by 4 May. Admiral Doenitz discusses surrender terms with Montgomery. On the 4th, a surrender document is signed, covering Holland, the German islands and Denmark. This surrender comes into force at 0800 on 5 May. The Danish resistance come out of hiding as the surrender is announced, taking over key buildings and communications. The Allies arrive on 5 May. The Russians are approaching Prague and Czech nationalists rise, capturing the main bridges over the Vltava river. The German garrison is ordered to smash the rebellion. On 7 May, the Germans sign an act of surrender, basically ending the war in Europe. Some 350,000 German troops surrender in Norway and the German army in Austria stops fighting on 7 May. On the Eastern Front, Prague is liberated on 9 May, and the Germans have given up fighting by 10 May, surrendering in their tens of thousands. The victorious allies begin to meet up, with the Russian 1st Ukranian Front meeting with the US Third Army on the Chemnitz-Rokycany Line on 10 May. There is still sporadic fighting and the last Germans surrender in the Balkans on 15 May. Shuri, Okinawa, is finally taken after some of the hardest fighting in the Pacific, on 29 May. The Americans have lost 20,000 troops in the fighting.

The Japanese have been defeated in Burma, but there are still 70,000 widely scattered Japanese troops throughout the country. The month of June is spent capturing and killing these ill-armed and almost starving troops. A month of hard fighting sees Okinawa cleared by 22 June. The Japanese commander on the island commits suicide that morning. In the 82-day fight for the island, he has seen 110,000 soldiers and sailors killed, along with 26,000 civilians. The Americans have lost 7,613 killed and 31,807 injured.

July sees a Japanese attack at Waw, using 6,000 men, the remaining soldiers of the Thirty-third Army, in an attempt to cut the railway line to Rangoon and to allow the Japanese Twenty-eighth Army to escape. By 11 July, the Japanese realize the attack is futile and give up. On 12 July, the Japanese initiate surrender talks with the Russians in Moscow. Moscow is not yet at war with Japan but the demands for unconditional surrender mean Japan continues to fight. Plans are in place for the final assault on mainland Japan, with plans for a seaborne invasion in November, and further assaults in March 1946. It is feared that the Japanese will fight to the death and that gains will involve hundreds of thousands of Allied casualties. However, unbeknown to many of the Allied commanders, the Americans have a secret weapon that may win the war early with few Allied casualties. On 16 July, they detonate the world's first atomic bomb at Alamogordo, New Mexico. The Manhattan Project, the top secret work to develop the bomb, using scientists from Britain, America and even ex-Germans, has come to fruition. American crews are already training to drop the bomb on Japan.

Between 17 July and 2 August, at Potsdam, the Allied leaders meet to discuss Japan and the rebuilding of post-war Europe. Japan is told that immediate surrender will see the Japanese nation continue but that the Empire would cease to be, war criminals would be arrested and tried, and that failure to surrender would see the 'utter devastation of the Japanese homeland'. The atomic bomb threat has been made. On 19 July, the Japanese Twenty-eighth Army tries to breakout from the Pegu Yomas but they are utterly decimated by Indian troops of the 17th Division. Hundreds are machined down, while many more drown in the River Sittang. The army is finished. The Japanese resistance in Mindanao is over on 26 July. The Japanese announce that they will ignore the Potsdam Proclamation on 28 July. The war with Japan continues.

August begins with the end of the Japanese Twenty-eighth Army on 4 August. The last survivors, who have chosen to fight to the death, are killed for the loss of just ninety-six Allied soldiers. On 6 August, a lone B-29 Superfortress takes off from Tinian Island and makes for Hiroshima. Enola Gay, as she is known, drops a single bomb on the city. It is the very first nuclear bomb dropped in anger and kills 70,000, destroying the city. The Japanese, having chosen to ignore the Potsdam Proclamation, are feeling the effects of their resistance.

On 9 August, the Russians attack Japanese forces in Manchuria. The 1.5 million Soviet troops attack the Kwantung Army, inflicted a speedy defeat on the war weary Japanese. On the same day, Japan feels the wrath of the Allies again. The high command had been warned that more bombs would be dropped and have chosen to ignore the Allies. The target this time is Nagasaki, and the shipyards and arms works of Mitsubishi. The pilot drops the bomb too early and it explodes a distance from the shipyards and the city centre. Hills shield the main city from the blast but 35,000 are killed and 60,000 injured. The next day, Japan surrenders unconditionally. The war is over. On 15 August, Emperor Hirohito announces that the Japanese people are to respond loyally to the surrender and give up their arms. In Manchuria, the Russians defeat the Japanese on 23 August, with 80,000 Japanese dead, and 594,000 now prisoners. The Russians have lost 8,000 dead and 22,000 injured.

Surrender is finally signed and sealed on 2 September aboard the USS *Missouri* in Tokyo Bay. The Second World War is officially over.

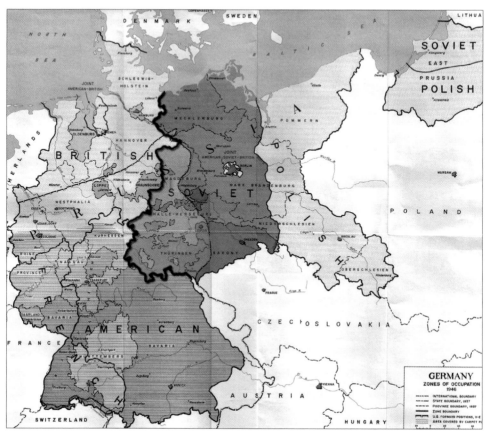

GERMANY
ZONES OF OCCUPATION
1946

INTERNATIONAL BOUNDARY
STATE BOUNDARY, 1937
PROVINCE BOUNDARY, 1937
ZONE BOUNDARY
U.S. FORWARD POSITIONS, V-E
AREA COVERED BY CARPET PL

Postscript to War

It is now that we should consider the cost of the seven years of war. Millions had died, Europe and large areas of Asia had been laid waste and would need rebuilt. Millions had become displaced and whole towns and cities destroyed. In numerical terms, the cost was huge. The Soviet Union came off worst, with around 7.5 million soldiers, sailors and airmen dead. The civilian toll was even larger with 15 million Russians dead, including many of the Jews and other ethnic minorities. Germany lost 2.8 million dead and 7.2 million wounded in the armed forces, with 500,000 civilian deaths. Japan lost 1.5 million troops, and 300,000 civilians, Italy suffered 77,000 military deaths and 40,000 civilian casualties. On the Allied side, the British lost 397,762 troops, the Americans 292,000, and the French 210,600. Civilian deaths included 65,000 in the UK and 108,000 French. Around 6 million Jews were among the 34 million civilian deaths worldwide.

The war left the world with two superpowers – Russia and the United States. It brought us the jet engine, the rocket and the nuclear bomb – all of which have changed the face of the world since. Politically, two opposing ideologies faced each other, bringing two one-time allies into conflict with each other, if only by proxy, as they each tried to control the world. The after effects included a splitting of Europe into two distinct zones – the West, essentially free, and the Eastern Bloc of Communist states, run by puppet leaders all answering to Stalin and the Soviets. Germany itself was split into two. In Asia, Britain lost much of its dominance and the jewels of its empire were made independent. The Allies splintered into pro-Soviet and pro-American groupings, seeing the rise of the military-industrial complex in the USA and in its NATO allies. The war itself had seen the rapid growth in technology that brought us jet airliners, satellites, nuclear power and improved technology in almost every field. It brought medical advances, improved communications, computers, microwaves and radar. The world had entered a brave new age but also one of fear and oppression for many. It had come as a direct result of the inadequate settlement for peace at the end of the First World War and continued where that one had ended. The century had seen some hundred or more million deaths, much of which achieved nothing in real terms. With luck, we may never see such a waste of human life again.

Opposite page, top: The immediate post-war programme of denazification saw the removal of all Nazi regalia and symbols, including named street signs. *(US DoD) Bottom:* A map showing the division of Germany into Allied Zones of Occupation, as decided at Postdam. *(LoC)*

From swords into ploughshares, ballistic rockets into Mickey Mouse. The race between East and West to grab Nazi technology saw many of the German engineers and scientists repatriated.

Top Left: A V2 rocket, abandoned in transit following Allied attacks on the railway network.

Bottom left: Wernher von Braun, the engineer behind Germany's rocket programme, poses with Walt Disney in 1959 during the making of a film entitled *Man in Space. (NASA)*

JANUARY 1945

Above: The German passenger ship *Wilhelm Gustloff* was torpedoed by the Soviet submarine *S-13* in the Baltic on 31 January 1945. She had been requisitioned by the Kriegsmarine in 1939 and initially served as a hospital ship before being reassigned as a floating barracks. In 1945 the ship was put into service as part of Operation Hannibal to evacuate troops and civilians from Courland, East Prussia and Danzig-West Prussia as the Red Army advanced. After being struck by three torpedoes the *Wilhelm Gustloff* toppled sideways, trapping many people in the freezing water. It is estimated that about 9,343 passengers and crew lost their lives, including around 5,000 children; the largest loss of life resulting from the sinking of a single vessel in maritime history.

V2 Attacks on London

By late 1944 the Luftwaffe's raids on London with conventional bombers were a thing of the past and many of the evacuated children had returned to the capital. Then, in September 1944, the V1 flying bombs and V2 rockets, Hitler's vengeance weapons, were unleashed to bring a new form of aerial terror to Londoners. The Allies' advance through northern France soon overwhelmed the V1 launch sites, but the V2s were a far more difficult target. Despite attempts by the Allies in January and February to destroy the launchsites, mobile rocket launch teams continued to evade attack by the RAF. The final two rockets fired against England came down in Orpington, Kent, on 27 March 1945, killing one civilian. Over 6,000 V2s were built, with around 3,225 launched. Although the V2s failed to change the outcome of the war, they accounted for approximately 6,000 deaths.

Top right: Clearing a few possessions from the wreckage from a V2 strike in Battersea on 27 January.

Bottom right: Locals take some comfort in a hot cup of tea served by a WVS canteen.

Opposite page: A boy with his stuffed toy amid the ruins. One of the most enduring images from the London Blitz, this 1945 photograph was taken by the American Toni Frissell, an official photographer of the US Women's Army Corps. *(Library of Congress)*

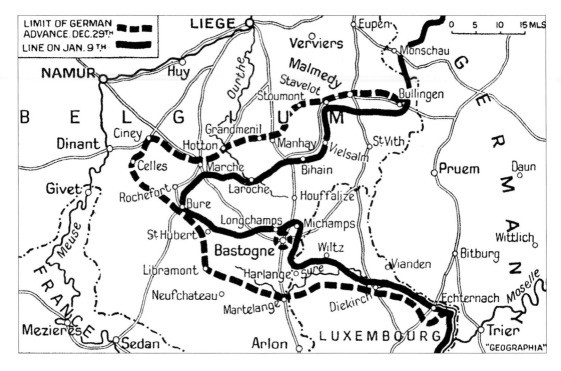

The Ardennes Offensive
Widely known as the Battle of the Bulge, this German counter-offensive against the Allies' advance in northern Europe had commenced on 16 December 1944 and continued until 25 January 1945. It was fought in the densely forested Ardennes region of Wallonia in Belgium, France and Luxembourg.

Above: A map of the area showing the extent of the Bulge on 29 December 1944, and the reduced area by 9 January 1945.

Left: A file of US prisoners captured by the Germans during the drive into Allied positions.

Above: Somewhere in the Ardennes, these Sherman tanks are directing their massed fire against the enemy's positions, with instructions received by the officer in the foreground. *Below:* An American infantryman passes the snow-covered bodies of German soldiers on the outskirts of the Belgian town of Grandmenil. Under Operation Greif the Germans successfully infiltrated a battalion of English-speakers wearing American uniforms behind the Allied lines.

From D-Day to the Rhine
Above: Shermans and infantry of the US 4th Armoured Division advancing through Coutances, which had been one of the first towns to be liberated following the Normandy landings. *(NARA) Below:* A knocked-out German tank on a road through the Hagenau Forest.

Above: Men of a British tank recovery unit take advantage of a break in the action to warm themselves around an improvised brazier. *Below:* Fog has been succeeded by almost Arctic-like conditions, as can be seen in this photograph of an anti-tank gun team on the River Maas front.

Top: The Belgian town of Bastogne was the scene of an engagement between American and German forces in late December 1944, during which it was heavily bombarded by the Germans. These photographs from January 1945 show some of the damage. *Below:* Montfort, in the Maas-Roer triangle, also shows the scars of war – mostly caused by Allied aircraft. It was captured by the British 2nd Army on 24 January.

Above: When troops of the British 2nd Army took Saffelen in the drive to straighten the lines between Geilenkirchen and Roermond, in the Netherlands, they came across this German sniper's nest perched at the top of two tall trees.

Heavy snowfalls in the Low Countries made the work of the RAF ground crews even more arduous. *Above:* Armourers brush snow from rows of 500-lb bombs ready for loading on to a North American B-25 Mitchell medium bomber. *Below:* Canvas tubes are used to pump hot air from a pre-heating van into the air intake of a Hawker Typhoon fighter-bomber.

There was also heavy snow in Britain. Shown above, all hands turn out to clear the snow from the runway and from the wings of an Avro Lancaster bomber.

Above: Field-Marshal Sir Bernard Montgomery photographed with several generals under his command on the northern flank of the Ardennes bulge. From left to right they are, General Sir Miles Dempsey, Major-General Hodges, Major-General Simpson and Lieut-General Crerar.

Left: The advance of the British 2nd Army to the east of Maeseyck and the Juliana Canal went steadily despite the bad weather conditions. Among the villages taken was Breberen, shown here.

Above: A Bren-Gun firing position inside a damaged house in Gennep. This city in south-eastern Netherlands was captured by British troops on 12 January 1945. *Below:* A mortar team of the US 7th Army fire over the German border from the neighbourhood of Lauterbourg.

Operation PLUTO – Pipelines to France
The problem of supplying prodigious quantities of fuel to the armies fighting in France was solved by PLUTO, the Pipe Line Under The Ocean. Developed by the Petroleum Warfare Department, the pipelines were laid on the bed of the English Channel. The first, laid on 12 August 1944, stretched for over 70 miles between Shanklin Chine, on the Isle of Wight, to Cherbourg. *Above:* HMS *Latimer* near the coast after laying the pipeline. *Below:* The pipe passing over a drum on *Latimer's* deck. By January 1945, 305 tons of fuel were being pumped to France every day.

Top: One of the PLUTO pipelines running out into the English Channel. *Middle:* Known as a Conundrum, or Conum, these huge steel drums carried the heavy 3-inch steel pipe and were towed across the Channel to lay a continuous length of pipe. *Bottom:* A Conum being moved into position to receive the pipe. Two lines were built, codenamed Dumbo and Bambi, and remained in operation until salvaged in 1946.

Through the Siegfried Line

Known to the Germans as the West Wall, this line of fortifications was meant to represent Germany's invulnerability, but in the event the Siegfried Line, a relic of the First World War, became a potent symbol of the Allies' unstoppable advance. Following a delay caused by the Ardennes Offensive, the assault on the Siegfried Line could begin and by late March 1945 it had been broken.

Top: US soldiers pass through one of the access gaps which had been blocked by the steel girders laid in the slots to either side. *Left:* A newspaper cartoon mocking Germany's faith in the West Wall, as they called it.

Auschwitz-Birkenau

This was a network of Nazi concentration/extermination camps consisting of Auschwitz I, Auschwitz II-Birkenau, and forty-five satellite camps. It is estimated that 1.1 million prisoners died at Auschwitz. Himmler ordered the evacuation of the camps in January 1945, and when the Red Army arrived on the 27th, only 7,500 prisoners and approximately 600 corpses remained. *Right:* Aerial photograph of the camp taken in 1944. The crematoriums are on the right. *Below:* Child survivors at Auschwitz. They are wearing adult-size jackets. *(US Holocaust Memorial Museum)*

AUSCHWITZ-BIRKENAU EXTERMINATION CAMP
OSWIECIM, POLAND
25 AUGUST 1944

War in the Pacific
Top: A line of US Coast Guard landing craft sweeping through the waters of Lingayen Gulf, carrying the first wave of Marines to the beaches of Luzon, 9 January 1945. *(NARA) Bottom:* A Japanese Type 95 Ha-Go light tank captured in Burma.

FEBRUARY 1945

Above: General de Lattre de Tassigny, Commander of the French 1st Army, inspecting units of the French Armoured Division which took part in the liberation of Colmar, during victory celebrations held in the city. The Colmar Pocket, in central Alsace, was cleared of German forces by the 1st Army by 9 February 1945.

Progress on the Eastern Front

Above: A Soviet tank passes along a street in the German Silesian town of Gleiwitz (now Gliwice, Poland) shortly after its capture on 24 January 1945. Much of the town had been set alight by the fleeing German forces as part of Hitler's scorched earth policy. Likewise, in Czestochowa the Soviets found that the town had been severely damaged by fire, shown below. In March 1945 Hitler issued the Nerobefehl, the 'Nero Decree', ordering the destruction of German infrastructure to prevent its use by the enemy. Fortunately, the man responsible for enacting the decree, Albert Speer, deliberately disobeyed the Führer.

In the West
Right: Map showing the
advance of the US 1st
and 9th Armies towards
Cologne, the capital
of the Rhineland and
Military Area Command
Headquarters, by
February 1945.

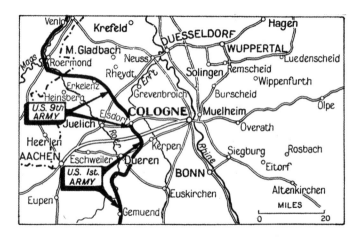

Above: Troops of
the British 2nd Army
footslogging through a
sea of mud following the
start of the thaw.

Right: This American
M10 tank destroyer has
taken up a well-concealed
position overlooking
enemy observation posts.
The M10 was christened
as the Wolverine by
the British, a name not
adopted by the American
soldiers.

Street fighting. *Above:* Infantrymen of the US 9th Army lie prone in the shelter of a low wall to avoid shell-fire in the battle-torn streets of Julich, which was cleared of German forces by 24 February. *Below:* Routing out enemy stragglers among the ruins of Prüem.

Above: A Beaufighter aircraft of the South African Air Force operating in the Balkans releases its rockets in an attack on the ancient castle town of Zuzuemperk in Yugoslavia.

The Yalta Conference

Between 4 and 11 February 1945, the 'Big Three' Allied leaders met at the Livadia Palace near Yalta in the Crimea to discuss Europe's post-war reorganisation. Shown above are British Prime Minister Winston Churchill, America's President Franklin D. Roosevelt and the Soviet Union's Premier Joseph Stalin. (This line-up was about to experience significant and unexpected changes in the ensuing months.) The main decision made at Yalta was to divide a defeated Germany into four zones of occupation, one each for the Big Three and a fourth smaller zone for France. Agreement was also reached on new governments for Poland and Yugoslavia.

The Battle of Iwo Jima
Above: US Marines pour ashore in the assault on Iwo Jima. *Below:* Coast Guard and US Navy landing craft deliver supplies on the blackened sands of Iwo Jima just a few hours after the initial landings.

Flamethrowers on Iwo Jima
New weapons were needed to deal with the countless foxholes and networks of caves from which the Japanese soldiers defended the Pacific islands. None were more effective than the flamethrower which fired a burning mixture of diesel fuel, gasoline and napalm jelly. It was a weapon of terror. *Left:* On Iwo Jima this US tank is equipped with a navy Mk 1 flamethrower based on the British Ronson system. *Main image:* A backpack flamethrower operator of the 9th Marines. The portable flame throwers had a range of around 65 feet.

The most iconic image from the Pacific Theatre is Joe Rosenthal's photograph of the raising of the flag at Iwo Jima (see colour section). *Right:* The flag flying on Mount Suribachi on Iwo Jima. *(NARA)*

Below: A Japanese 12-inch gun captured by US troops of the 158th Regimental Combat Team in the hills near Rosario, on Luzon in the Philippines. *(NARA)*

The Battle of Manila
Japanese forces had been ordered to resist to the last man, and General MacArthur's troops are shown during mopping-up operations in the Philippines capital. The battle for Manila had begun on 3 February and was concluded on 4 March, at enormous cost to the city.

MARCH 1945

The senior American commanders of the Second World War. Seated from left to right: Generals William H. Simpson, George S. Patton, Carl A. Spatz, Dwight D. Eisenhower, Omar Bradley, Courtney H. Hodges and Leonard T. Gerow. Standing, left to right: Generals Ralph F. Stearley, Hoyt Vandenberg, Walter Bedell Smith, Otto P. Weyland and Richard E. Nugent. Before the year was out, George S. Patton would die as the result of a road accident. *(NARA)*

In March the Prime Minister Winston Churchill paid a vist to the American 9th Army, which was part of Field Marshal Montgomery's 21st Army Group. *Top:* He is shown viewing the ruins of Juelich with General Simpson, C-in-C of the 9th Army. *Bottom:* Amid the concrete dragon's teeth of the Siegfried Line at Vaals, accompanied by Montgomery, Field-Marshal Sir Alan Brooke and General Simpson.

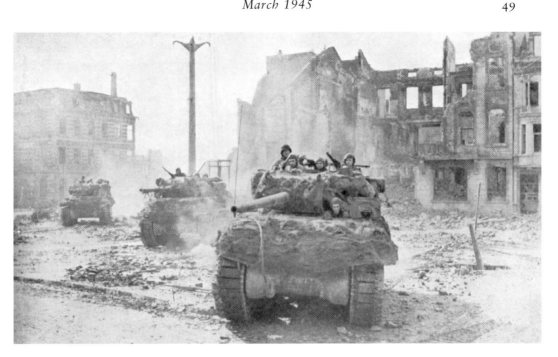

Above: American 9th Army tank-destroyers entering the industrial city of Muenchen-Gladbach (Mönchengladbach) west of the Rhine, which was captured on 1st March 1945. *Below:* A German mother and her children look on as an American soldier maintains a firing-point on a street corner in Neuss, occupied by the US 9th Army on 2 March.

The Grand Slam Bomb
Officially designated as the Bomb, Medium Capacity, 22,000 lb, the Grand Slam was a scaled-up version of the Tallboy earthquake bomb designed by Barnes Wallis. Entering service in March 1945, almost at the end of the war, Grand Slams were dropped on a number of targets within Germany.

Top: This range of RAF bomb types goes from 500 lbs up to the Grand Slam's 22,000 lbs.

Left: The warhead has been filled with high explosives. After release the Grand Slam achieved near-supersonic speed, 715 mph, and would detonate deep underground to cause maximum damage.

Above: A Grand Slam being handled at RAF Woodhall Spa. It is 35 feet 5 inches long, with a diameter of 3 feet 10 inches. *Below:* A 12,000-lb bomb being hoisted into the belly of a Lancaster. The heavier Tallboy and Grand Slam were carried by the Lancaster B Mk 1 (Special).

The Ludendorff Bridge at Remagen

Above: In early March 1945, this was one of only two remaining useable bridges across the Rhine. On 7 March troops of the US Army's 9th Armoured Division reached the railway bridge and were surprised to find it still standing despite Hitler's orders that it should be destroyed at the last minute following the Germans' retreat. *Below:* Anti-aircraft gunners keep watch for enemy aircraft.

Above: American engineers of the US 1st Army work to strengthen the strategically important railway bridge at Remagen, which was in a perilous state. Note that planking has been laid over the railway tracks to allow road vehicles to cross. The Allies were able to transport six divisions across the Rhine before the bridge collapsed on 17 March, only ten days after it had been captured, killing eighteen US Army engineers. The bridge was not rebuilt after the war.

Crossing the Rhine
Above: A floating pontoon bridge across the Rhine. The width of the river and its fast-flowing waters made such crossing points a difficult task for the army engineers.

Opposite page: A US mortar crew in action near the Rhine, and soldiers under enemy fire as they cross the river at Goar in March 1945. 'I drew an assault boat to cross in – just my luck. We all tried to crawl under each other because the lead was flying around like hail!'

Top: Accompanied by Field-Marshal Sir Bernard Montgomery and General Simpson, Commander US 9th Army, Winston Churchill crosses the Rhine in an American LCVP (Landing Craft Vehicle, Personnel). Also known as a Higgins boat, more than 20,000 of these versatile landing craft were built during the war. *Bottom:* The British prime minister is shown observing the Rhine operation from the east bank at Wesel.

Top: Soldiers of the US 7th Army at a roadblock on the main street of Güdingen, near Saarbrüken, which was captured on 16 March. *Bottom:* US Army vehicles crossing the River Prüm at Lünebach in March 1945. *(NARA)*

Left: A German Jagdtiger, a Hunting Tiger, put out of action by American Thunderbolt aircraft. The Jagdtiger was a heavy tank-destroyer based on a lengthened Tiger II chassis. The heaviest armoured vehicle of the war, it entered production in 1944 and only eighty-eight were built by the end of hostilities.

Middle left: German stragglers being rounded up and marched through the market square in the university city of Heidelberg, which was captured by the Allies on 30 March 1945. The city had escaped bombing during the war as it was not an industrial centre or a transport hub. The US Army chose Heidelberg as a garrison base.

Bottom left: General Eisenhower and Allied officers view bodies at the Ohrduf forced labour and concentration camp on 12 April, eight days after the camp's liberation. *(NARA/ USHMM)*

Attack on USS *Franklin*

Above: The USS *Franklin*, with USS *Sante Fe* alongside, on 19 March 1945, following an attack by a Japanese aircraft. *Below:* The view from the *Sante Fe*, showing the aircraft carrier listing badly. Many of the crew are on the deck – 724 lost their lives in the fire, but the ship did not sink and was taken in tow for repairs at Pearl Harbor. Commissioned in January 1944, she had served in several of the Pacific campaigns and was decommissioned in February 1947.

The Devastation of Manila

The capital of the Philippines was taken by the Japanese in January 1942, following extensive bombing. It was retaken by US and Filipino troops in one of the bloodiest battles of the Pacific Theatre from 3 February to 3 March, resulting in the death of some 100,000 civilians. Here are two views of the devatation inflicted on Manila. *Above:* Downtown. *Below:* An aerial view of the walled city of old Manila, photographed in May 1945. *(NARA)*

APRIL 1945

Above: US Navy LSM(R) – Landing Ship Medium (Rockets) – firing rockets in the Kreama Islands in March 1945, during preliminary action prior to the commencement of the Battle of Okinawa on 1 April. The eighty-two-day battle lasted until 22 June. The 188-Class LSM(R)s were equipped with eighty-five Mk 51 automatic rocket launchers in addition to their conventional armaments.

Death of President Roosevelt

On 12 April 1945 America's longest-serving president, Franklin Delano Roosevelt, shown above left, died suddenly in Warm Springs, Georgia, while sitting for a portrait. Despite a decline in his health, the death of the sixty-three-year-old came as a shock to the entire world. In Germany Hitler greeted his sudden death as a divine intervention and Goebbels described it as a sign of a turning point in the Nazis' darkest hour. As the news filtered though to the US servicmen at the front, many refused to believe it and put it down to German propaganda. *Above right:* His Vice President, Harry S. Truman, took the oath of office that same day and would dedicate the victory in Europe to his memory. *Below:* Funeral procession in Pennsylvania Avenue. *(LoC)*

Operation Iceberg – The Okinawa Landings
Above: Landing craft on the beachhead on the western coast of Okinawa, 1 April 1945. The amphibious landings, known as Operation Iceberg, saw 160,000 US troops put ashore. They faced minimal reistance at first, but this intensified as the action moved inland. *Below*: US Marines pass through a small village littered with the bodies of the Japanese soldiers. *(NARA)*

The Italian Offensive

Above: The 8th Army opened a new offensive across the Senio river on 8 April. Infantrymen moving through barbed wire defences on the southern bank of the Senio. *Below:* Churchill tanks in action, assisting with harassing fire against German positions on the Italian front.

Above: Tanks, troops and a mule of the US 5th Army, 10th Mountain Division, move forward near Bolgona on 14 April. The animals provided an invaluable means of transporting supplies in the more difficult mountainous terrain. Large numbers of mules used by the Allies during the advance through Europe. Germany in particular made extensive use of horses and mules, with an estimated 2.75 million employed during the course of the war.

Right: Gunners of the 92nd Division enter the Galleria Guiseppe Garibaldi in the newly liberated city of Genoa. *(NARA)*

Allied Armour in Germany

Above: American troops catch a lift on a British Churchill tank passing through the village of Appelhulsen on the way to Muenster (Munster). *Below:* An American Motor Carriage M18 tank-destroyer in action in support of infantry attacking Wiesloch. Known as the Hellcat, the M18 was one of the few wartime tanks not based on the Sherman chassis. The M18 was armed with the 76-mm M1 gun and saw action in Europe from the summer of 1944 onwards.

Above: Two of the Allies' ubiquitous M4 tanks, christened the Sherman by the British. These tanks of the 3rd Armoured Division of the US 9th Army are shown entering the town of Lemgo as some of the civilians wave white flags. *Below:* An M18 of General Patton's 3rd Army enters the square of the Thuringian town of Gotha. This had been a centre of the arms industry during the war with an estimated 7,000 forced labourers working in the armaments factories.

The Liberation of the Netherlands
Famed more for the ill-fated Operation Market Garden's attempt to secure the bridge at Arnhem, in September 1944, the town itself was liberated between 12 and 16 April 1945 as part of the Canadian First Army's Operation Anger, which was led by British and Canadian armoured divisions. *Above:* With fires burning, British troops deal with fierce resistance in Arnhem.

Right: A Canadian
soldier stands beside a
bullet-ridden signpost
in Holland in April
1945. The German
word *Gesperrt* means
blocked or inaccessible.
Note that Wieringen,
in the north-west and
shown as 29 km away
on the signpost, was
cut off by the Allied
advance and not
liberated until 8 May.
(National Archief)

Bottom right: Food
drops were organised
to alleviate the
shortage of food for
those people stranded
in the Nazi-occupied
north-west. Here,
the bomb-bay of a
Lancaster bomber
is being loaded with
food supplies. These
drops were carried out
from 29 April until
8 May 1945, under
an agreement made
with the German
commander that the
aircraft would not
be fired-upon within
specified air corridors.
Some 11,000 tons of
food was dropped by
this means.

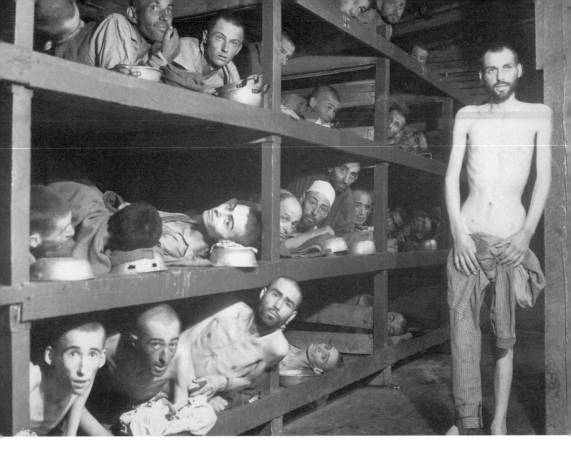

Buchenwald

One of the largest concentration camps on German soil, Buchenwald consisted of several subcamps. The first to be liberated was Ohrdruf, by US 89th Infantry Division on 4 April. However, in the days before complete liberation, thousands of prisoners were forced by the Germans to join evacuation marches, and it wasn't until 11 April that the main Buchenwald camp was entered by members of the US 9th Armoured Division, part of the US 3rd Army. The following day, several journalists arrived. This extract is from Edward R Murrow's broadcast for CBS:

> I asked to see the barracks. It happened to be occupied by Czechoslovaks. When I entered, men crowded around, tried to lift me to their shoulders. They were too weak. Many of them could not get out of bed. I was told this building once stabled eighty horses. There were 1,200 men in it, five to a bunk. The stink was beyond all description.

Above: Slave labourers at Buchenwald, photographed five days after their liberation. *(NARA)*
Opposite page, top: Buchenwald's crematorium represents slaughter carried out on an industrial scale. One estimate places the number of deaths, including some POWs, at around 56,000.
Bottom: Senator Alben W. Barkley, a member of a Congressional team investigating Nazi atrocities, views a pile of bodies. Barkley later became vice president under Truman. *(NARA)*

East Meets West
The highly symbolic meeting of
American and Soviet troops took
place at Torgau, on the River
Elbe, on 25 April 1945 – a date
now celebrated as Elbe Day.

Left: 2nd Lieutenant William
Robertson, of the US Army, and
Lieutenant Alexander Silvashko,
of the Red Army, embrace at an
offical photo-op. The meeting of
the forces advancing from the
west and the east meant that the
Allies had cut Germany in two.

Below: More staged handshakes
at Torgau.

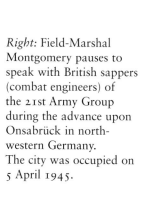

Above: A captured German Tiger I tank being examined by men of the 8th Army. Equipped with the 88-mm gun, this heavy tank saw action on all German battlefronts from 1942 until the end of the war.

Right: Field-Marshal Montgomery pauses to speak with British sappers (combat engineers) of the 21st Army Group during the advance upon Onsabrück in north-western Germany. The city was occupied on 5 April 1945.

Above: Nuremberg, famed as the scene of the mass Nazi Party rallies before the war, fell to US troops on 20 April 1945. A Sherman tank is firing point blank at buildings to take out German snipers holding up the advance into the city. *Below:* In Italy the US 5th Army entered Genoa on 27 April. The city had been liberated by the partisans a few days before their arrival.

Deaths of the Great Dictators
Right: The Stars and Stripes for
2 May 1945, reporting the death
of Adolf Hitler. Just after midnight
on 29 April Hitler had married Eva
Braun in a civil ceremony held in
the Führerbunker. Later that day he
learned of the death of Mussolini,
and, determined to escape a
similar fate, on 30 April he shot
himself after Braun had bitten into
a cyanide capsule. Their bodies
were taken up to the bombed-out
garden of the Reich Chancellery,
doused with petrol and burned
with the Red Army closing in only
a block or two away. *The Stars
and Stripes*, the daily newspaper
for US servicemen, was published
in several editions to cater for the
different theatres of war.

Below: The bodies of Benito
Mussolini and Clara Petacci, and
other executed Fascists, hanging
from meat hooks in Milan.

The aftermath. *Above:* Köln, or Cologne, lies in ruins in April 1945 with almost every building destroyed. The city had been a Military Area Command Headquarters and was extensively bombed. To the east of the cathedral, the Hohenzollern Bridge is in ruins. *(US DoD) Below:* Just some of the hundreds of thousands of German prisoners taken during the Allied advance into the Reich. Many would suffer extreme hardship, especially those in the hands of the Russians.

MAY 1945

With the war against Germany drawing to its close, attention would shift to events in the Pacific where the fighting would continue for another three months. *Above:* A US Marine Corps Chance Vought F4U-1D of the Marine Fighter Squadron at Kadena, Okinawa. Better known as the Corsair, the F4U had been designed as a carrier-based fighter aircraft, but was also used extensively by the Marines as a land-based aircraft. Over 12,000 were built, many by other manufacturers Goodyear and Brewster to meet the demand. It went on to see service in the Korean conflict.

Denmark Freed
Top left: Celebrating the liberation of Denmark in the streets of Copenhagen on 5 May 1945. Around 6,000 Danes were sent to concentration and labour camps during the war, and many others were imprisoned or killed for resisting the German authorities. *(National Museum of Denmark)*

Bottom left: Thousands of Danes lined the streets to welcome Field-Marshal Montgomery when he visited Copenhagen on 12 May.

The Fall of Berlin

Above: Raising the Soviet flag above the Reichstag building, an iconic photograph taken during the Battle of Berlin on 2 May. *Below:* Many Germans stayed in the beleagured city, hiding in cellars and bunkers. Following the surrender they attempted to resume their lives amid the ruins of a shattered Berlin, and they are shown clearing rubble from the Unter Den Linden.

Above: Amid the ruins of Hitler's 1,000-year Reich, the battered shell of the Reichstag in Berlin. An anti-aircraft gun stands in front, its barrel still pointed skywards. *Below:* Wrecked vehicles and armoured cars in the courtyard of the Reich Chancellery.

Two photographs of the
Reich Chancellery taken
by an American
serviceman, Melvin C.
Shaffer, in May 1945.
'The famous bunker was
here and the smell of death
emanated from every
direction. We searched for
any remains of Hitler and
photographed the entire
structure. The Russians
showed us where the body
of Hitler had been
burned ... The area smelled
of gasoline and burnt
flesh.'

Right: Looking up into
what had been the dome
of the main hall. *(Southern
Methodist University,
Central University
Libraries, DeGolyer
Library)*

The German Surrender

Above: The German peace envoy walk to Montgomery's headquarters at Luneberg Heath on 4 May. This was the surrender of the German forces in the Netherlands, north-west Germany and in Denmark, and naval vessels in those areas. Among the group are General Admiral Von Friedeburg, General Kienzel, Rear-Admiral Wagner, Colonel Pollek and Major Friedel. *Below:* The final surrender took the form of two signing ceremonies, one in Rheims on 7 May, and another definitive surrender signed in Berlin on 8 May, shown here, with Wilhelm Keitel signing the Act of Military Surrender.

Above: General Jodl, central between Major Wilhelm Oxenius and General Admiral Von Friedeburg, signing the surrender at Rheims on 7 May. *Below:* Senior Allied commanders celebrate at Rheims after the signing. Left to right are General Ivan Susloparov of the Soviet Union, Lieutenant General Frederick E. Morgan of the British Army, Lieutenant General Walter B. Smith (US Army), Harry H. Butcher (US Navy), Dwight Eisenhower and Air Marshal Arthur Tedder of the RAF. *(NARA)*

Only this text in English is authoritative

ACT OF MILITARY SURRENDER

1.　We the undersigned, acting by authority
of the German High Command, hereby surrender
unconditionally to the Supreme Commander, Allied
Expeditionary Force and simultaneously to the
Soviet High Command all forces on land, sea, and in
the air who are at this date under German control.

2.　The German High Command will at once
issue orders to all German military, naval and
air authorities and to all forces under German
control to cease active operations at 2301 hours
Central European time on 8 May　　　　and to
remain in the positions occupied at that time.　No
ship, vessel, or aircraft is to be scuttled, or any
damage done to their hull, machinery or equipment.

3.　The German High Command will at once
issue to the appropriate commanders, and ensure
the carrying out of any further orders issued by
the Supreme Commander, Allied Expeditionary Force
and by the Soviet High Command.

4.　This act of military surrender is without
prejudice to, and will be superseded by any
general instrument of surrender imposed by, or
on behalf of the United Nations and applicable
to GERMANY and the German armed forces as a whole.

- 1 -

The instrument of the German surrender, signed on 7 May 1945 at Eisenhower's headquarters
in Rheims. It was signed on behalf of Germany by Alfred Jodl, Chief of Staff of the German

5. In the event of the German High Command or any of the forces under their control failing to act in accordance with this Act of Surrender, the Supreme Commander, Allied Expeditionary Force and the Soviet High Command will take such punitive or other action as they deem appropriate.

Signed at *Rheims at 0241* on the *7th* day of May, 1945.
France

On behalf of the German High Command.

Jodl

IN THE PRESENCE OF

On behalf of the Supreme Commander,   On behalf of the Soviet
Allied Expeditionary Force.   High Command.

W. B. Smith   *Susloparov*

Sevez -2-

Major General, French Army
(Witness)

Army, in the presence of W. B. Smith, on behalf of the Allied Supreme Commander, Susloparov, for the Soviets, and it was witnessed by Major General F. Sevez of the French Army.

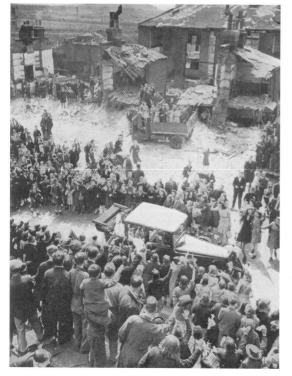

VE Day

Above: In London huge crowds gathered in front of Buckingham Palace to greet the king and queen, the two princesses and Winston Churchill when they emerged on the balcony to acknowledge their cheer on Victory in Europe Day, 8 May 1945.

The king and queen had worked tirelessly during the war, lending their support and encouragement both to the armed forces but also those who lived and worked on the home front. During the Blitz they became regular visitors to those affected and earned the admiration of a generation by refusing to leave London. *Left:* There was little let up in their schedule in 1945, and they are shown visiting areas of the East End that were damaged by the V2 rocket attacks. The Royal car is passing through a blitzed street in Deptford.

For those in the armed forces, the news that the war had ended was spread by various means. *Above:* British troops cluster around a radio to hear Field-Marshal Montgomery's announcement of the surrender of Germany's forces in Holland, north-west Germany and Denmark. *Below:* In the square at Weiden in Germany, American soldiers listen to an announcement by General John Leonard, Commander of the 9th Armoured Division, on 9 May.

Above: On 7 May, while men of the 6th British Armoured Division were held up in their advance into Austria by road demolitions, two German officers arrived to seek surrender terms. *Below:* New Zealand troops in Italy examine a wrecked German tank.

Top left: On 6 May, Reich-Marshal Hermann Göring surrendered himself to the US 36th Infantry Division at Radstadt in the Salzburg area. He is shown still wearing his sky-blue uniform. *Top right:* Dr Robert Ley, leader of the German Labour Front, following his arrest. Both men would be tried for war crimes at Nuremberg. *Bottom:* Field-Marshal Von Rundstedt, the former supreme commander of the Western Front, was captured at his Bavarian retreat. Charged with war crimes, he did not face trial due to his age and poor health.

The End of Germany's Navy
Two photographs showing the extent of the devastation inflicted on Germany's shipyards. *Top:* U-Boat bow sections stand in the foreground, and behind them the upturned keel of the heavy cruiser *Admiral Von Scheer*, sunk by RAF Tallboy bombs on 9 April 1945. *Bottom:* The cruiser *Köln* rests on the bottom of the dock at the naval base at Wilhelmshaven.

Above: Surrendered destroyers anchored up at Kiel. *Below:* Ammunition being unloaded at Copenhagen on 18 May during the disarming of the cruisers *Prinz Eugen* and *Nürnberg*. German naval ratings are unloading ammunition from the *Nürnberg*.

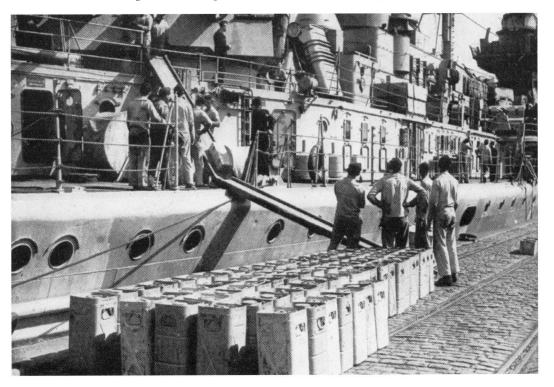

Some of Germany's small ships and craft that had been operating in the Adriatic were brought into Italian ports after the surrender. *Top:* A *Vorpostenboot*, or flakship. These smaller vessels modified for use in combat were mostly used for coastal patrols and ship escort duties. *Middle left:* Hoisting the White Ensign on board an E-boat. *Middle right:* Royal Navy officers inspecting a flakship. *Bottom:* A German hospital tender.

Above: The crew of the *U-249* coming aboard a Royal Navy vessel. The *U-249*, a Type VIIC U-Boat launched in October 1943, was one of the first of the German submarines to be surrendered and she came into Weymouth harbour on 10 May, flying the black flag of surrender. Under Operation Deadlight, *U-249* was scuttled off Northern Ireland in November 1945. *Below:* More surrendered U-Boats, this time in the lock at Wilhelmshaven harbour.

On 13 May two German E-Boats, or *Schnellboots*, meaning 'fast boats', were escorted into Felixstowe harbour, shown above, by ten British MTBs (Motor Torpedo Boats). Heavily armed, the E-Boats could sustain 43.5 knots and briefly accelerate to 48 knots. *Below:* On board one of the E-Boats that came into Felixstowe was Rear-Admiral Bruening, commander of the E-Boat operations. He is being saluted as he was piped ashore to sign the Instrument of Surrender.

Three E-Boats that were escorted to Portsmouth from Den Helder in Holland. Each had a crew consisting of one officer and nine men, shown coming ashore in the lower photograph. The indentations on either side of the bow are in front of the openings for two torpedo tubes.

Hundreds of aircraft were surrendered by the Luftwaffe. *Above:* US soldiers can be seen viewing some of them. Among them it is possible to identify examples of the Messerschmitt Me 109 and Bf 110, and a Focke-Wulf Fw 190. On the far left there is even a Messerschmitt Me 262 jet – see page 122 for more on these. *Below:* German trucks stretching as far as the eye can see.

Above: The 'Big Three', Churchill, Roosevelt and Stalin, gathered at Yalta on 11 February 1945 to discuss the division of Germany into controlled zones. It would be their last meeting as President Roosevelt, *below left*, died suddenly on 12 April after serving less than three months of his fourth term. He was succeeded by his Vice-President Harry S. Truman, *below right*.

Clearing Britain's Beaches

With the threat of invasion finally over, the retrictions governing access to the beaches could be removed and from early 1945 work commenced on clearing anti-invasion obstacles, including the mines. In the *top* photo, mines are being exploded on a beach under supervision of Sappers of the Royal Engineers. It was dangerous work and a number of men died in the course of this clearance operation. *Bottom:* Bringing recovered mines through the barbed-wire defences.

Buchanwald Concentration Camp
These harrowing photographs from the liberation of the Buchenwald concentration camp are a poignant reminder of the depth of Nazi depravity. Located near Weimar in central Germany, it had been established in 1937 as one of the first and largest of the camps on German soil. Prisoners from all over Europe and the Soviet Union were taken to Buchanwald to work as forced labour in the local armaments factories. It was not a death camp as such, although it is estimated that over 56,000 prisoners died there. Buchanwald was liberated by the US 89th Infantry Division on 4 April 1945. Among them was Lieutenant Parke O. Yingst, who took these photographs of emmanciated survivors and of the heaps of corpses. After the war the camp was used by the Soviets as Special Camp No. 2, and it is thought that between 1945 and 1950 a further 7,113 inmates – mostly opponents of Stalin – died there. *(US Army and US Holocaust Memorial Museum)*

Above: 'The Big Three will tie the enemy in knots.' A Soviet cartoon by Kukryniksy. *Below:* The moment when the Germans surrendered unconditionally their forces in western Europe to Field-Marshal Montogomery at 21st Army Group HQ on Lüneburg Heath, 4 May 1945. Montgomery is shown reading the terms to Admiral von Friedeburg and Rear Admiral Wagner.

Above: The Military Government assumed control of Berlin on 12 July 1945 and Field-Marshal Montgomery represented the British at a ceremony at Brandenburg Gate. He is shown here after investing Marshal Zhukov and Marshal Rokossovsky with the British KCB. *Below:* An official map showing the division of occupied Germany into four zones of occupation

The Lights Go Back On

On 10 May, two days after Winston Churchill's broadcast announcing that the war against Germany was over, Britain's blackout restrictions were lifted and public buildings in London were floodlit once more. A system of half lighting – the 'dim out' – had been introduced in September 1944 and this had been extended to normal lighting from 23 April 1945. *Above:* The Middlesex County Council building in Parliament Square being half-lit, and the clock tower of the Houses of Parliament in the floodlights that signalled the return to peace and normality.

Left: London's Victory Parade, which was held on 8 June 1946. The king took the salute of the Empire and Allied forces in the Mall, and here the Civil Defence section is shown passing the Houses of Parliament before entering Whitehall.

Above: Poster for the July 1945 general election, in which the Labour Party secured a landslide victory, ousting Winston Churchill as prime minister and replacing him with Clement Attlee.

The Battle of Iwo Jima

The American invasion and capture of the four-mile island of Iwo Jima, to the south of Japan, with its strategically important airfield, saw some of the fiercest fighting of the entire Pacific campaign. Following naval shelling and aerial bombardment of the heavily-fortified island, the 4th and 5th Marine Divisions made an amphibious assault on the beaches. Despite intense artillery fire from the entrenched Japanese forces, the US had 30,000 men on the island by the end of that first day. The Battle of Iwo Jima has been imortalised by Joe Rosenthal's photograph of the raising of the US flag on the top of Mount Suribachi, taken on the fifth day of the action. This iconic image, shown opposite on a war loans poster, was actually the second raising of a flag on this spot. Three of the Marines featured in the photograph were killed in action over the next few days. The fighting on Iwo Jima continued until 26 March. Of the 22,000 Japenese soldiers defending the island, only 216 were taken prisoner and the majority of the others were killed in action.

Left: Three US Navy photographs showing the landing on Iwo Jima.

Opposite: 7th War Loan poster featuring Joe Rosenthal's iconic photograph, *Raising the Flag on Iwo Jima.* The photograph won the 1945 Pulitzer Prize for Photography. *(LoC)*

7th
WAR LOAN
NOW··ALL TOGETHER

Left: General Douglas MacArthur was Field Marshal of the Philippine Army and Supreme Commander, Southwest Pacific Area. He officially accepted Japan's surrender on 2 September 1945 – see opposite – and oversaw the occupation of Japan from 1945 to 1951. He later led the United Nations Command in the Korean War. *(US Navy)*

Below: The New-Mexico Class battleship USS *Idaho* is shown shelling the island of Okinawa, 1 April 1945. Previously, the *Idaho* had blasted enemy positions as the US Marines stormed ashore at Iwo Jima before taking part in the Battle of Okinawa, which was to be the last of the great assaults of the Pacific war. *Idaho* entered Tokyo Bay on 27 August and was anchored there during the signing of the Japanese surrender on board the *Missouri* on 2 September. She was decommissioned in July 1946 and placed in reserve until sold for scrapping in November the following year.

Right: On 2 September 1945, the Japanese representatives arrive on the USS *Missouri* in Tokyo Bay to sign the formal Japanese Instrument of Surrender. The ceremony lasted twenty-three minutes and was broadcast throughout the world. The documents were first signed by the Japanese foreign minister, Mamoru Shigemitsu, on behalf of the Emperor and the Government. Then, General Yoshijiro Umezu, the Chief of the Army General Staff, shown below, takes up the pen and adds his signature. *(NARA)*

Right: Douglas MacArthur, Commander of the Pacific and Supreme Commander of the Allied Powers, accepted the Japanese surrender and signed on behalf of the Allied powers, followed by a further nine Allied delegates from the USA, China, UK, Soviet Union, Australia, Canada, France, the Netherlands and New Zealand. MacArthur is shown here, signing the documents. *(NARA)*

Mass Destruction
Top left: The Kölner Dom, the Cologne Cathedral, stands seemingly undamaged while the surrounding area is devastated, photographed here in April 1945. The destruction of many of Germany's cities as part of the Allies' strategic bombing campaign was achieved through conventional, almost industrialised, mass-bombing raids, but the dawn of the Atomic Age brought a new level of instant destruction. *(US DoD)*

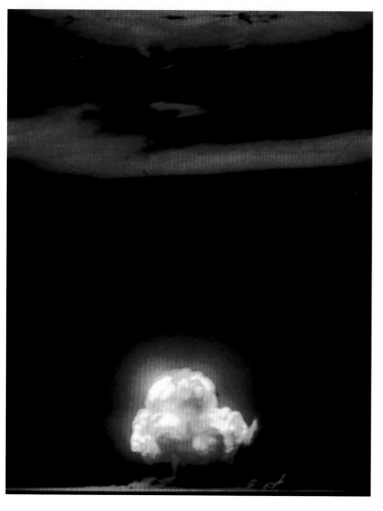

Bottom left: Preliminary tests in the Manhattan Project to develop an atomic bomb were carried out on the Alamogordo bombing range in New Mexico. This photograph was taken on 16 July 1945 and shows the detonation of the first atomic bomb as a mushroom of smoke and flame rises to a height of 40,000 feet. *(US Army)*

The B-29 Super Fortress
Designed by Boeing as a high-altitude strategic bomber, the B-29 was one of the most advanced aircraft of the Second World War and was used exclusively in the Pacific Theatre. After the war it continued in service, seeing action in the Korean conflict, until it was retired in 1960. The first aircraft to drop the atomic bomb on Hiroshima, on 6 August 1945, was the *Enola Gay*. Shown above is *Bockscar*, which dropped the second bomb, called Fat Man, on Nagasaki three days later. *(National Museum of the US Air Force)*

Right: 'Build More B-29s' poster. *(LoC)*

Atlantic Victory

On 6 June 1945, President Truman and Winston Churchill issued their last statement on the war against the U-boats. They described it as 'a long struggle, demanding not only the utmost courage, daring and endurance, but also the highest scientific and technical skill.' The convoy system had played an important part in the struggle, notably in the Atlantic and on the Murmansk route to Russia. During the war, around 75,000 merchant ships were escorted across the Atlantic in 2,000 convoys.

Left: Two photographs of a wartime convoy under escort in the Bay of Biscay.

Above: A US Navy K-ship class blimp on patrol. Such non-rigid airships had been used with great success on anti-submarine maritime patrols by the British in the First World War. The K-ships were much bigger. They had a crew of nine or ten, and with a maximum endurance of thirty-eight hours they had a potential range of 2,200 miles. 135 were built by Goodyear and operated mostly over the Atlantic and Pacific, although a contingent was sent via the Azores to Europe, where they operated out of Morocco over the Mediterranean. In July 1943, K-74 was lost when it was shot down by U-134. Some continued in service after the war and the last was retired in 1959. *(US Navy)*

Right: A poster for the United Nations, the organisation established in the immediate aftermath of the war on 24 October 1945. As a replacement for the League of Nations, its role was to promote international co-operation and prevent another global conflict. *(LoC)*

UNITED NATIONS

We, 1,750,000,000 People

for understanding—for peace

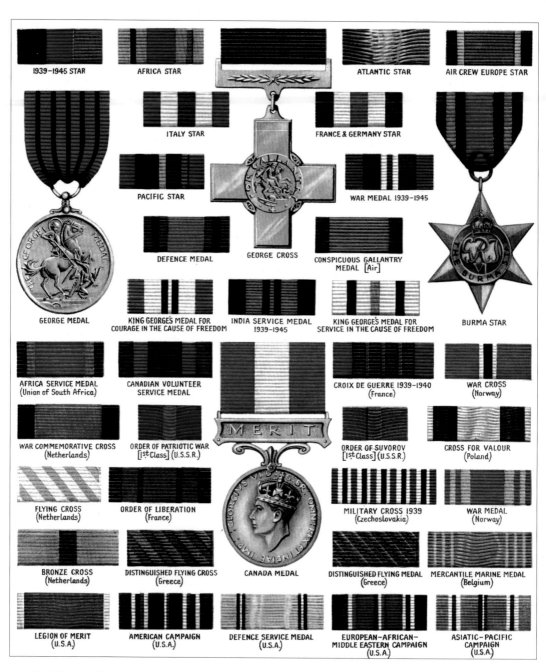

British Awards and Decorations of the Second World War

Eight British Campaign awards were approved by the king during the war. They were: 1939–45 Star, Africa Star, Atlantic Star, Air Crew Europe Star, Burma Star, France and Germany Star, Italy Star and the Pacific Star. The design of the stars were similiar to the Burma Star shown here on the top right. Also approved were the War Medal 1939–45, the India Service Medal 1939–45, and the Defence Medal. The George Cross and George Medal had been instituted in September 1940, primarily to reward acts of gallantry by civilians arising out of enemy action, although there was also a small Military Division of the Cross. Ribbons of representative Dominions and Allied awards are also shown here.

Admiral Karl Dönitz was appointed as Führer following the death of Adolf Hitler, and on 2 May the new Government Executive of the Reich fled to Flensburg, near the Danish border, with headquarters in the naval academy in Mürwik. This government was dissolved on 23 May when Dönitz, along with Albert Speer and Alfred Jodl, shown above, were taken into captivity. All three would appear at the Nuremburg trials. *Below:* Heinrich Himmler's attempt to join the Flensburg government was rejected by Dönitz, and after being captured on 21 May he committed suicide by means of a cyanide capsule, shown below. The two men in the upper left are the bodyguards captured with Himmler.

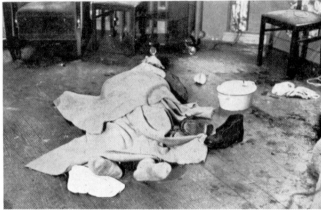

The War in the East
Rangoon, the capital of Burma, was finally captured on 3 May 1945 after a series of actions against the Japanese. *Top:* Indian tanks and infantry in action in Burma. *Bottom:* Around 1,700 American-built M3 Lee and Grant medium tanks were sent to south-east Asia and were used extensively by the British 14th Army for infantry support in the fighting around Rangoon.

The Battle of Tarakan
Top: Australian infantrymen landed on Tarakan, Borneo, on 1 May, in an operation code-named Oboe One. *Bottom:* Australian-manned Matilda IIs coming ashore from the American landing craft. The British Matilda II Infantry Tank had been designed at the Royal Arsenal, Woolwich, before the outbreak of war and most were built by the Vulcan foundary in Newton-le-Willows, Lancashire. In the Pacific Theatre it saw service with several Australian regiments.

These photographs show former prisoners held by the Japanese in appalling conditions. *Above left:* A Canadian surgeon with three of his fellow prisoners, including one whose leg he successfully amputated. *Above right:* Liberated prisoners take their last meal of rice before being moved to a base camp. *Below:* These prisoners were abandoned by the Japanese during their retreat from Burma.

Top right: Matilda tanks on Labuan Island off the coast of Borneo. This was a prime objective for the Allies as it was being used by the Japanese as an administrative centre.

Middle right: Two Australian soldiers move steadily forward on the captured airstrip following the 10 June landings. Most of the island was under their control within four days.

Bottom right: A Japanese train captured in a rail siding during the Allied advance on Rangoon.

Okinawa

Fighting on the Ryukya Islands on Okinawa, which had started at the beginning of April, continued right through May 1945.

Top left: A stranded US Sherman awaits the arrival of towing equipment.

Lower left: A Marine of the 2nd Battalion, 1st Marines, on Wana Ridge on 18 May, firing a M1 Thompson submachine gun.

Below: A demolition crew of the 6th Marine Division watch the explosion of a dynamite charge placed in a Japanese-held cave on Okinawa. *(NARA)*

Above: Republic P-47 Thunderbolt fighters in RAF colours on a forward airstrip on the Arakan front in south-west Burma. A Boeing B-29 bomber can be seen in the background. *Below:* This RAF reconnaissance squadron operated in Burma using Hawker Hurricanes. On the left the camera is shown being prepared for loading into the underside of the fuselage.

US Aircraft in the Pacific
Above: A Corsair fires its rockets on a run against the Japanese on Okinawa. *(NARA)*

Opposite page, top: A US Marine Corps Grumman F6F-5N Hellcat launched from the deck of USS *Block Island* off Okinawa, 10 May 1945. *Opposite page, bottom:* Four Goodyear-built FG-1D Corsairs of the Marine Fighter Squadron VMF-323 on a rocket strike against Japanese positions. *(US Navy)*

Above: B-29s dropping incendiary bombs on Yokohama. *Below:* A dramatic view looking down on one of the American bombers over Osaka on 1 June 1945.

Top: Tokyo's wooden buildings are engulfed by fire after a B-29 firebomb raid on the city on 26 May 1945. The aftermath of the fires is shown in the bottom image. *(LoC)*

Kamikazes Strike USS *Bunker Hill*
Dramatic images of the USS *Bunker Hill*
billowing smoke off Kyushu after being
struck by two Japanese kamikaze aircraft in
thirty seconds on 11 May 1945.

Above: The destroyer USS *Charles S. Sperry*
is alongside fighting the fire. *Right:* smoke
billowing from *Bunker Hill*. *Below:* A view
of the flight deck. The ship's aircraft had
not been launched at the time of the attack.
Over 300 men died in the fire, but the
Bunker Hill did not sink and she limped
to the Philippines for initial repairs before
returning to the USA. *(NARA)*

Clearing up Hitler's Mountain Retreat
Top: A working party of Nazi prisoners is put to work in clearing up at Berchtesgaden in the Bavarian Alps. Hitler's mountain residence, the Berghof, was located here and in April 1945 it was damaged by Allied bombing raids. *Bottom:* Devastated by the bombing, the ruins of the Berghof had little to offer visiting US soldiers in the way of souvenirs.

The first garden party to be held at Buckingham Palace since before the war took place, on 24 May 1945, when the king and queen were hosts to nearly 2,000 newly returned prisoners of war. *Below:* Princess Elizabeth looks on as her father enjoys a joke with some RAF officers.

JUNE 1945

Above: The US Navy Gato-class submarine USS *Barb* departs from Pearl Harbor on 8 June 1945 on her twelfth patrol. USS *Barb* is credited with sinking seventeen enemy vessels, including the Japanese aircraft carrier *Unyo*. Launched in April 1942, the *Barb* went on to serve until December 1954 when she was transferred to the Italian Navy and renamed *Enrico Tazzoli*. She was sold for scrap in 1972.

It wasn't only the servicemen who were trying to get home. It is estimated that millions of DPs – Displaced Persons – including refugees, forced labourers, internees and displaced Germans, were on the move in 1945. Many were fleeing the advancing tide of the Red Army when Germany was carved up into the four zones of occupation. This was the greatest movement of people in history. *Above:* Freed Russian slave workers disembarking from a train near Luneburg and boarding the British trucks that will take them to the Russian lines in the Baltic.

Above: Liberated British POWs were transported back to the UK in their thousands. These men are boarding a Lancaster for the trip home. *Below:* Some of the former prisoners displaying their war trophies at a reception centre in Southampton.

On 12 June 1945, General Dwight D. Eisenhower was at the Guildhall in London to receive the Freedom of the City. After the ceremony he went to the Mansion House, where he spoke from the balcony as shown above.

Above: Men of the Royal Artillery ack-ack units arrive at the Military Collecting Unit, Duke of York Headquarters, Chelsea, prior to demobilisation. The process had begun in June 1945 and over the next eighteen months about 4.3 million men and women returned to civvy street. *Below:* Soldiers of the 8th Army leaving Calais on the last lap of their journey home.

Troop-Carriers
Top left: The German liner *Europa* was taken over for war service. After being repaired at Bremerhaven, she would be used as a troop-carrier taking US troops back across the Atlantic.

Middle left: A photograph taken from an RAF Coastal Command aircraft of the *Aquitania*, the White Star liner which, together with her sister-ships *Queen Mary* and *Queen Elizabeth*, was on active service as a troop carrier. This was the second war seen by the *Aquitania* and she remained in service until 1950.

Bottom left: Some of the 15,000 American personnel homeward bound on the *Queen Elizabeth*. This dormitory for 300 men had been converted from the ship's observation lounge.

Above: Still wearing her grey war-paint, the *Queen Mary* arriving in New York on 20 June 1945, with thousands of American soldiers on board. Note the degaussing coil around the hull. This device was used to decrease a ship's magnetic signature and thus reduce its vulnerability to magnetic mines.

Right: US troops returning from Europe pack the decks of the *Queen Mary* as she steams into New York harbour.

Evidence of Germany's desperation was found in the scrap yards of occupied Europe, where all types of metal objects had been gathered. These photographs were taken in a smelting yard in Hamburg and show bronze statues and church bells heaped up ready for smelting.

An aerial photograph of a depot near Munich showing hundreds of B-17 Flying Fortresses lined up. Some of the aircraft would join the war in Japan along with the 8th Army Air Force, but the majority would be scrapped. After the war the B-17 was quickly phased out of use.

War Winning Technology

It was only with the end of the war that some of the secret technology deployed by the victors could be revealed, and the best example of this was radar. Sir Stafford Cripps stated that, 'radar, more than any other scientific factor, contributed to the final victory over Germany'. *Above:* An airwomen is plotting aircraft on a cathode-ray tube. Over 4,000 WAAF personnel took an important part in the operation of the radio-location equipment.

Left: The Bernard/Bernhardine radio-navigation was used by the Germans to assist their fighter aircraft with the interception of Allied bombers. This is the Bernard VHF rotating directional-beacon being shown to RAF technicians by Luftwaffe personnel. The Bernhardine Hellschreiber unit in the aircraft printed the data stream to provide the pilot with information to make an intercept.

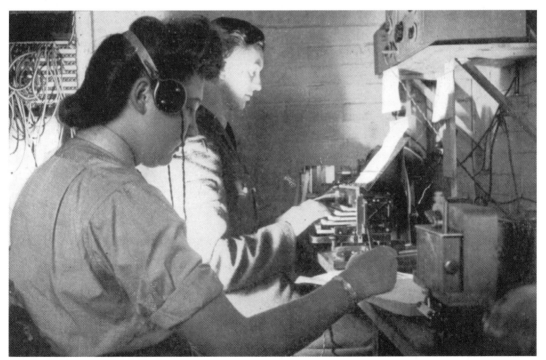

The RAF's meteorological organisation also played a vital role in the air war. In the pre-satellite age information was gathered by radio-sonde balloons, shown top left, and at ground stations, shown top right. *Bottom:* A WAAF checks a radio transmission of weather forecasts from the Central Forecasting Station while an aircraftman prepares a tape message.

War Prizes – German Aircraft

At the end of the war the Allies vied with each other to grab as much of the Nazi technology as possible, especially the jets and rockets. *Above:* An Me 262A-1a surrendered at Frankfurt in March. *Left:* This wooden-framed He 162 *Volksjäger*, the people's fighter, was captured in France. *Below:* Arado Ar 234 *Blitz* bomber wearing British markings.

Right: Dornier's Do 335 was one of the most unusual aircraft of the war. Known as the *Pfeil*, or Arrow, it featured a unique push-pull configuration with two Daimler-Benz DB 603A piston engines, making it the fastest heavy fighter in the Luftwaffe's arsenal. But only a handful were delivered before the war ended.

The Germans also developed rocket-powered aircraft as rapid interceptors against the waves of Allied bombers. *Above:* A Messerschmitt Me 163B Komet at an RAF airfield in England. *Right:* The Bachem Ba 349 *Natter*, or Viper, was a vertically launched interceptor.

Above: American soldiers at the camouflaged south entrance to the Mittelwerk weapons factory. This extensive facility under the Harz mountains, near Nordhausen, had been carved out from an existing anhydrite mine by an army of slaves. Here, the inhabitants of the Dora concentration camp worked in horrendous conditions to construct the V1 and V2 vengeance weapons. *Middle left:* Many of the V2 rockets were left stranded on the railway network following Allied air raids. An American soldier examines the tail end of a V2. *Bottom left:* Germany also exported its technology to Japan. This is an *Ohka*, a one-man flying bomb based on the V1, the Fieseler Fi 103R. Nicknamed by the US troops as a 'Baka', the Japanese word for fool, it was found on Okinawa.

Germany's rocket technology was very advanced and was used to power a range of sophisticated weapons, including guided missiles.

Top right: At BMW's rocket development department at Bruckmühl, Rosenheim, a German engineer shows a BMW 109-558 liquid-fuelled rocket to a member of a British techinical investigation team. This rocket motor was developed for the Henschel Hs 117 *Schmetterling* (Butterfly) ground-to-air missile.

Middle right: A British intelligence officer examines an Hs 293 anti-shipping glide bomb fitted with a Walter 109-507B rocket motor. The Hs 293 was dropped from an aircraft and remotely guided to its target by a controller. It is credited with sinking and damaging a number of Allied ships from 1943 onwards.

Bottom right: The *Hecht*, or Pike, was an experimental surface-to-air missile under development by Rheinmettal-Borsig.

Above: Japanese pilots receiving instructions before the start of a bombing raid. *Below:* A tracery of anti-aircraft fire from the Marine defenders of Youtan airfield on Okinawa.

Above: Private First Class Tony Dixon uses an abandoned barber's chair to cut the hair of Sergeant John Anderson near Shuri, Okinawa, 10 June 1945. *(NARA)*

Right: With the captured capital of Okinawa, Naha, in the background, Marine Major General Lamuel Shepherd, the commanding general of the 6th Marine Division, relaxes on Okinawa Ridge to consult a map of the terrain. *(NARA)*

Above: Japanese prisoners held at Okuku, on Okinawa.

Left: There is no mistaking the abject dejection of this Japanese prisoner behind the barbed wire. *(NARA)*

JULY 1945

Above: These Spitfire pilots are part of two RAF squadrons operating from an advanced base in Burma to provide support to the army. Here they are seen crossing a rain-sodden airfield after returning from a sortie.

The British in Occupied Berlin

Top: On 19 July, large flights of war pigeons were released on their last assignment for the British. Some carried messages for the Princess Royal and the Chief of the Royal Signal Corps, while others carried them for Bayeux, Brussels, The Hague and Venio. *Bottom:* A NAAFI mobile canteen in front of the Brandenburg Gate. The Navy, Army and Air Force Institutes ran 7,000 canteens with 96,000 personnel by 1944. It also controlled ENSA – Entertainments National Service Association – the forces entertainment organisation.

The Union Jack flies in front of the 1870 Victory Memorial in the Koenigsplatz as the Canadian Composite Battalion pipe band marches during the British Berlin Victory Parade held on 21 July. This is not to be confused with the Berlin Victory Parade held by the four main Allies on 7 September. One man's victory is the other man's defeat, and for the Berliners these parades must have been humiliating.

Top: Field-Marshal Montgomery escorts Marshal Zhukov on an inspection of a Guard of Honour of the 1st Grenadier Guards in Berlin. *Bottom:* Afterwards Montgomery presented Marshal Zhukov with the CGB and Marshal Rokossovsky the KCB in front of the Brandenburg Gate in recognition of the Soviet contribution to the Allied victory.

One of the tasks that befell the Allies in occupied Germany was sorting out the treasures accumulated in the Reichsbank. *Top right:* A US officer assists a Treasury expert from New York in evaluating the miscellaneous valuables.

Middle right: One of the strong rooms is stacked with gold bars and bullion worth millions.

Bottom right: The Allied scheme for feeding the German population of Berlin saw tons of powdered milk, flour, fats and potatoes sent over from the UK. Here, trucks have been loaded with potatoes at Spandau West Station in Berlin.

The Potsdam Conference

The final wartime meeting of the Big Three, *above*, took place at Postdam, in occupied Germany, from 17 July to 2 August 1945. Its purpose was to decide how to administer punishment to Germany and establish a post-war order.

Left: The USS *Philadelphia* leading the cruiser *Augusta* which brought President Truman to the conference. He landed at Antwerp, drove from there to Brussels and then flew to Potsdam.

Opposite page, top: the three leaders and their staff gather around the table at Postdam. Taken on 19 July, this photograph shows Stalin at the top, with Churchill and Truman to either side near the bottom. Clement Atlee is also shown, two up from Churchill who he would shortly replace as British Prime Minister.

Opposite page, bottom: The three leaders pose before taking their seats.

The General Election
On 5 July 1945 Britain
went to the polls to elect a
new government to replace
the wartime coalition. In
a shock result the Labour
Party won a landslide
victory, putting Clement
Attlee in Downing Street as
prime minister.

Left: This election poster
plays heavily on the need
to give the returning
servicemen homes and
work.

Bottom left: The results
were not counted and
declared until 26 July. This
edition of *Picture Post*,
published on 11 August,
marks the Labour victory
with an image of smiles
in the sunshine. The dark
years of the war were
behind them and it was
time to look to the future.

The Pacific War
Above: Japan's light cruiser *Oyodo* viewed from an American aircraft flown for the carrier USS *Wasp*. The *Oyodo* capsized in shallow waters near Kure on 28 July 1945 after being hit by eight 500-lb bombs in four days. *(US Navy)*

Above: A damaged Curtiss SB2C-4E Helldiver of Bomber Squadron 87, on the deck of the aircraft carrier USS *Ticonderoga. Below:* A Vought F4U-1/FG-1 Corsair crashes in flames on USS *Essex.* The aircraft's belly fuel tank had broken loose during landing. *(US Navy)*

AUGUST 1945

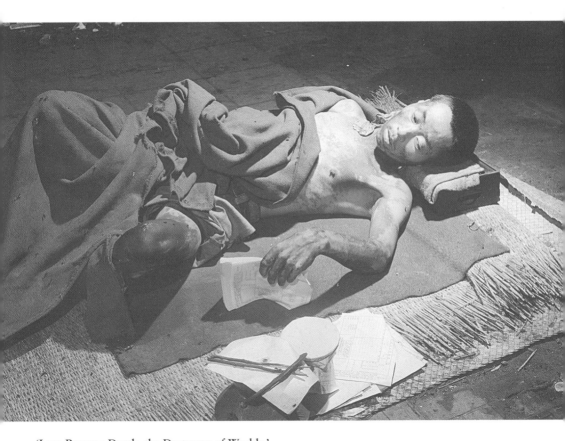

'I am Become Death, the Destroyer of Worlds.'
Above: A victim of the bomb that fell on the Japanese city of Hiroshima at 8.15 a.m. on
Monday 6 August 1945. After that moment the world would never be the same.

Opposite page:
Colonel Paul W.
Tibbets, Jnr, pilot of
the *Enola Gay*, the
B-19 Super Fortress
which dropped the
atomic bomb on
Hiroshima. He is
shown shortly before
taking off on the
mission, about six
hours' flight time
from the target. The
Enola Gay was named
after Tibbets' mother.
(NARA)

*Top right: The
Knoxville News-
Sentinel* of 6 August
announces the atomic
strike. Oak Ridge
was one of the sites
for the Manhattan
Project which saw the
development of the
atomic bomb.
(Energy.gov)

Bottom right: The
mushroom cloud
billows up to 20,000
feet above Hiroshima.
Between 70,000 and
80,000 people were
killed in the blast and
ensuing firestorm.
(NARA)

Above: The *Enola Gay* landed back at base on Tinian after the strike. *Enola Gay* acted as a weather reconnaissance aircraft on the second mission, with the primary target of Kokura. However, clouds and drifting smoke, from the firebombed city of Yawata, resulted in Nagasaki being bombed instead.

Left: The Little Boy bomb on a trailer cradle at Tinian, prior to being loaded into *Enola Gay*'s bomb bay. It was the first atomic bomb to be used in warfare, and the Hiroshima bombing was only the second artificial nuclear explosion in history, after the Trinity test on 16 July 1945. *(NARA)*

Above: Fat Man was the codename for the implosion-type bomb dropped on Nagasaki on 9 August. It was dropped by a B-29 Superfortress called *Bockscar*, so named after its pilot, Captain Frederick C. Bock. It is shown below at Tinian on the day of the atomic mission.

Opposite: A second mushroom cloud over a Japanese city in three days. The bomb was detonated at an altitude of 1,800 feet above Nagasaki and the two images on this page show the extent of the bomb's destructive force. *Below:* The shell of the Catholic church. *(NARA)*

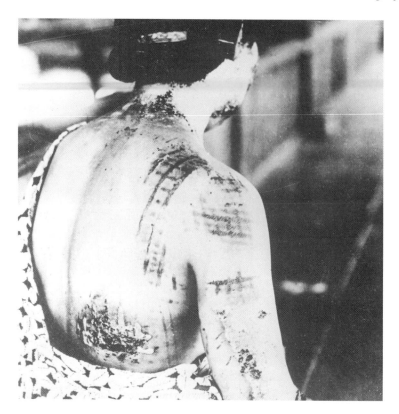

Left: A victim of the bomb at Hiroshima, this woman's skin has the burned-in pattern of the dark portions of the kimono she had been wearing. *(NARA)*

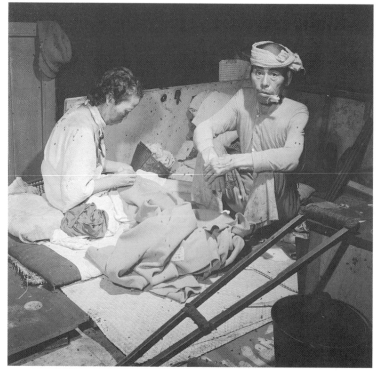

Bottom left: Blast victims find shelter in the fly-infested hospital set up in a bank building. *(NARA)*

Above: In a crowded Oval Office at the White House, President Harry S. Truman reads the announcement of the Japanese surrender to reporters. *(NARA) Below:* Residents of Oak Ridge, one of the main sites of the Manhattan Project responsible for refining uranium, celebrate the ending of the war. *(US Army)*

V-J Day in Times
Square, New York,
14 August 1945.

Above: Thousands of
New Yorkers gather in
the square to celebrate
an end to the war.

Left: One of the most
iconic moments of the
entire war, if not the
twentieth century as
an American sailor
spontaneously grabs
a girl and kisses her.
This photograph
was taken by US
Navy photographer
Victor Jorgensen and
captures the same
scene also snapped
by Alfred Eisenstadt
and published in *Life*
magazine. *(NARA)*

POSTSCRIPT TO WAR

Above: Welders at Ingalls Shipbuilding Corporation yard in Pascagoula, Mississippi. The war had seen countless thousands of women on both side of the Atlantic working in the armaments factories, but with the coming of peace many of these jobs would disappear as the men came home.

Japan Signs the Surrender

Above: Thousands of spectators, photographers and film cameramen fill every vantage point on USS *Missouri* in Tokyo Bay as they await the arrival of the Japanese delegation on 2 September 1945. VJ Day is more than two weeks earlier, on 15 August, to mark Emperor Hirohito's radio broadcast announcing the surrender which, in effect, ended the Second World War. *(US DoD)*

Above: The Japanese delegation arrives aboard the *Missouri*. The figure holding the stick and wearing a top hat is Foreign Minister Mamoru Shigmitsu, with General Yoshijiro Umezu, Chief of the Army General Staff, standing by his side. *Below:* General Douglas MacArthur, as Supreme Allied Commander in the Pacific, signs the Instrument of Surrender. It was also signed by representatives from the other Allied countries. The ceremony lasted twenty minutes and formalised the surrender of the Empire of Japan. *(NARA)*

Left: Back from the Far East, three members of the crew of HM submarine *Trident*. They are holding one of the flags they found in a landing craft that they had attacked. A British T Class submarine built by Cammell Laird and launched in December 1938, she was broken up for scrap in 1947.

Bottom left: One of the thousands of servicemen returning to civilian life, this former RAF man is being fitted with his demob suit at the Demobilisation Clothing Depot. Clothing rationing meant that it was not possible to buy a new suit from a shop. The need to deal with such large numbers of men meant that the suits all looked the same and many did not fit well, and consequently the demob suit become the butt of countless jokes.

Above: The coming of peace meant the return to normality, and for this young ATS girl that meant back to her life as a princess. The future Queen Elizabeth had joined the ATS as a mechanic at the age of eighteen and is shown here dressed in overalls changing a wheel at an ATS Training Centre in Camberley.

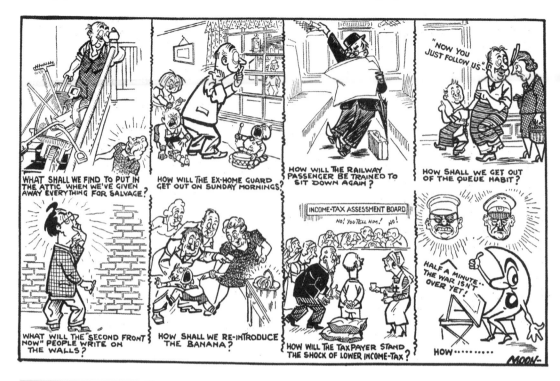

Above: 'Post-War Problems.' This wartime newspaper cartoon anticipates the joys and tribulations of the coming peace. Everything from the Home Guard stuck at home with his howling kids, to less crowded trains and the need to get out of the habit of queueing. In truth these changes wouldn't come overnight and some forms of rationing, for example, continued for several years after the war had ended.

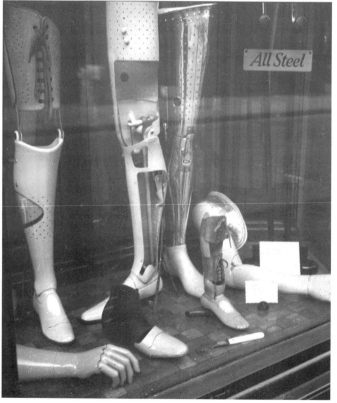

Left: This shop window display, photographed in London in 1946, is a sobering reminder that for many people the war would have a lasting impact upon their lives. *(Stockholm Transport Museum)*

Above: In the aftermath of the war, a York aircraft of RAF Transport Command is being serviced at Luga airfield during a regular passenger service and freight-carrying flight from England to the Far East. *Below:* It wasn't only German aircraft that were taken by the Allies as war prizes – see page 122. These Japanese aircraft are being prepared for shipment at Yokosuka in October 1945. The USS *Barnes* will take them to the USA for appraisal. *(SDASM)*

Above: Preparing the courtroom inside the Palace of Justice at Nuremberg. *Below:* Guards leaving the cell block area inside the prison that will hold the Nazi prisoners. *(US Army)*

The Nuremberg Trials

Aside from the distribution of Germany's territories, the Allied leaders meeting at Potsdam also had to agree on how to proceed with the prosecution of the Nazi war criminals. It was decided that the leading figures, or at least those who had not evaded capture, were put on trial at the Palace of Justice in Nuremberg in November 1945. The most prominent of the accused were Hermann Göring, the former head of the Luftwaffe; Rudolf Hess, Hitler's former deputy; Joachim von Ribbentrop, the German Foreign Minister; Wilhelm Keitel, Chief of the German Armed Forces; Karl Dönitz, Grand Admiral and Hitler's nominated successor as Führer; Erich Raeder, former Grand Amiral, Baldur von Schirach, Head of the Hitler-Jugend (Hitler Youth) and Fritz Saukel, General Plenipotentiary for Labour Deployment. Others included Ernst Kaltenbrunner, Alfred Rosenberg, Hans Frank, Wilhelm Frick, Julius Streicher, Walther Funk, Hjalmar Schacht, Alfred Jodl, Franz von Papen, Arthur Seyss-Inquart, Albert Speer, Konstantin van Neurath and Hans Fritzsche. Additional trials were held for the Nazi doctors and judges.

Sentencing did not take place until 1 October 1946. Twelve of the defendants were sentenced to death, including Göring who evaded the hangman's noose by taking cyanide. The executions took place in the gymnasium of the court building and the bodies incinerated at a crematorium in Munich.

Below: Robert Jackson, the US Chief Prosecutor, presents evidence to the court in the case against the defendants. *(USAMHI)*

Above: The senior Nazis in the dock at Nuremberg. From left to right: A slimmed-down Hermann Göring sits in the front row; Rudolf Hess, Hitler's former deputy; Joachim von Ribbentrop, the German Foreign Minister; and Wilhelm Keitel, Chief of the German Armed Forces. Back row: Karl Dönitz, Grand Admiral and Hitler's nominated successor as Führer; Erich Raeder, former Grand Amiral; Baldur von Schirach, Head of the Hitler-Jugend (Hitler Youth); and Fritz Saukel, General Plenipotentiary for Labour Deployment. Continuing to the right and out of camera beyond the aisle were Ernst Kaltenbrunner, Alfred Rosenberg, Hans Frank, Wilhelm Frick, Julius Streicher, Walther Funk, Hjalmar Schacht, in the front row, plus Alfred Jodl, Franz von Papen, Arthur Seyss-Inquart, Albert Speer, Konstantin van Neurath and Hans Fritzsche, in the back row.

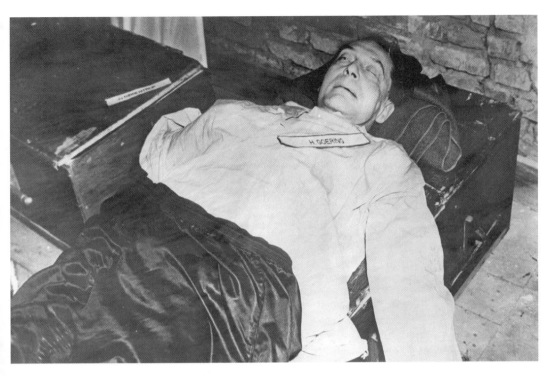

Above: The body of Hermann Göring on 16 October 1946. Sentenced to death, he escaped the hangman's noose by comitting suicide with a potassium cyanide capsule the night before he was to be hanged. *Below:* Wilhelm Keitel was hanged on 16 October 1946.

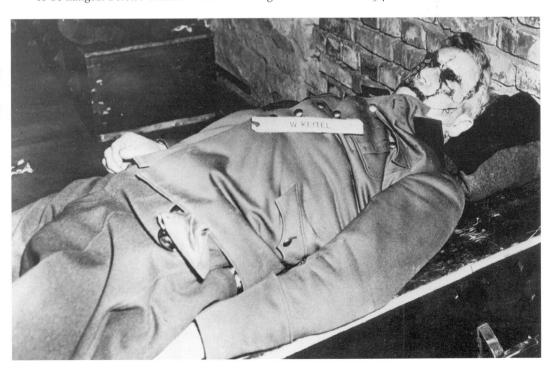

'And now let's learn to live together.'
A 1945 newspaper cartoon published in the *Daily Mirror*.